From Vegas to the Pearly Gates

A gritty, true life account of love at its best and absolute worst

Wendy Harrington

This edition, published by Gilhespy Publishing, 2016

A catalogue copy of this book is available from the British Library.

Typeset by Gilhespy Publishing.

Cover Design by Ignacia Ruiz
www.ignaciaruiz.com

Paperback ISBN - 978-0-9956376-0-3
ePub ISBN - 978-0-9956376-1-0

Contents

Dedication

For my beautiful daughters: Katy, Amy and Martha.

You bring me unbridled joy and I am so proud of you all.

Acknowledgements

Special thanks to the medical and hospital staff who provided such incredible care, encouragement and support. Especially Mr Inglefield, Kevin Williams and the team who dared to do the impossible in order to give me the chance to live.

Heartfelt thanks to my Mum and my sister Ruth, your ceaseless belief in me, support, love and selfless giving gave me the strength to carry on. I could not have done it without you.

Big thanks to my special friend Rachel who was a wonderful source of support for this book, by reading drafts and nudging me to keep going.

Thank you to every single person who has helped me and touched my life on this incredible journey so far.

Most of all Ro, without your hand I would not have been here to make this incredible journey and be sharing this story.

And finally for all my lovely friends who have encouraged me by continuing to ask "When will it be ready, I want to read it." Here it is!

Chapter 1
Written in the Cards

September 1999

I was at work and one of the girls was raving about this woman she had seen for a tarot reading. This was all a bit new to me but as she was so excited about how accurate this lady was and the clarity and direction it had given her it felt very appealing. I was at a crossroads in life, married with two small children and bored out of my mind. I loved my girls Katy, aged four and Amy, aged two very much but something was missing in our marriage. I felt unappreciated and really unhappy. I found myself flirting with another man at work and felt a real pull towards him. I felt guilty and confused and I thought that maybe a tarot card reading might be just the thing to help me focus and find the right way forward.

My main focus was my marriage and this new man. What should I do? I booked an appointment and went along for my reading. As the lady began talking about other stuff, I wasn't really that interested. Plus, I didn't know then what I know now – hindsight is indeed a wonderful thing. She gestured towards my lower abdomen and said, "You have a large black area there. It's Mother issues and if you don't deal with them you'll be ill." At the time this went in one ear and out the other. I wasn't interested in issues or emotional healing. I didn't know about energy and I also didn't give much weight to other people's ability to 'see' energetically, either. Even the idea that our bodies hold our pain and angst was an alien concept to me, let alone the fact that you could do something about it. I could have prevented an illness occurring, but I didn't realise it then. Was it a warning? *Undoubtedly*. Could I have done anything about it? *Maybe...* But we cannot change the past, only learn from it and hope to do things differently in the future. I was only interested in the best choice for my intimate relationship. This was my life's obsession; in finding 'the one' and having the perfect relationship and loving family of my dreams. The reading didn't give me the clarity I had hoped for. She said it was my choice to make which, of course, is correct.

I left the session still feeling confused. The connection I felt with this new man was incredible. He was called Roland, although everyone called him Ro, and I found him irresistible. It was like the draw of a magnet that I could not stop even if I wanted to. I did try to stay and make a go of things with my marriage; I had two delightful small children and this felt like the thing I 'should' do… but the only thing that made me *really* sad was the thought of not being with Ro. I remember asking him, "Are you going to take on me AND my two children?" Without hesitation he replied a resounding, "Yes." The way I felt about him was like nothing I had ever experienced before. I fell in love with my first husband in the beginning all head over heels, on cloud nine – all those glorious metaphors – but with Ro it was out of this world. It wasn't long before I broke off my marriage and left with the girls. It was a tricky period, filled with guilt and judgement. Understandably my husband was very angry and upset and my family were certainly not happy with me either. Inevitably, there was the split of friends that happens when a marriage breaks down yet, for me, as long as I was with Ro I didn't care, it made it all bearable. He was true to his word and fully embraced the girls like he said he would, like they were his own. His playful spirit meant that they quickly loved him too. Our new family shared many lovely times filled with laughter. We had lots of fun. I felt like I was alive after a long period of sleep, and that, as long as we had each other all was well in my world.

I became pregnant quite soon after we got together and we were both delighted. In April 2001 when I was five months pregnant, the two of us went to Las Vegas for a holiday and got married. We didn't tell a soul and had the most beautiful day. We were really happy and looking forward to the new addition to our family.

3rd June 2001

I'm 32 weeks pregnant and all is going well. The extension into the loft has gone smoothly, so we now have more space, which is great. We are just finishing decorating the hallway, which means the house will be completed ready for our new arrival in eight weeks. I'm feeling very excited!

"Phew, this glossing takes ages, doesn't it," I remark to Ro. Moments later a rush of heat flushes through me and I suddenly feel really sick. I take a deep breath and stop. "You okay, love?" Ro asks, looking concerned. "No, I feel really sick. I'm going to lie down for a bit. Probably too many gloss fumes."

I make my way to the bed and collapse onto it. I really don't feel well with a cramping tummy and feeling hot. I'll just sleep for a bit I think then I'll be fine. I close my eyes but it's very hard to sleep. My stomach is cramping so much. I go and try to make myself sick… I'll spare you the details but let's just say it's minimal; probably some sort of stomach bug and hopefully I'd feel better by the morning. I was trying to convince myself this was the case.

4th June 2001

After a fretful night I was still feeling really poorly and the cramping had worsened. Ro took the girls to school before taking me to the doctor. As I explained the symptoms to the doctor he said that he was sure it was okay. However, as a precaution he wanted me to go to the maternity unit to be monitored. I was a little worried but was sure it would all settle down as we made our way to the hospital. When we arrived they immediately rigged me up to monitor the baby's heartbeat. They also gave me an injection to promote the baby's lungs, just in case it was born early. They reassured me that 32 weeks was viable.

I lay in the bed and relaxed as much as I could. I felt mad at myself for every thought I'd had about wishing the baby would hurry up. I didn't *want* the baby to hurry up now! I wanted it to stay safe and sound where it should be, in my womb for another eight weeks. It was Amy's fifth birthday the next day and I didn't want to miss that for her. I lay there wishing that everything would all settle down and I would be able to go home soon.

The baby's heartbeat was steady all afternoon and the cramps/contractions subsided. I was really glad. They kept me in overnight, mainly because they needed to give me a second injection for the lung development quite late in the evening. I wanted to go home because of Amy's birthday; I wanted to be there in the morning to wish her happy birthday and share in her excitement. I persuaded the doctor to let me go home first thing the next morning and I promised to come back after the school drop off. This way I could still see Amy and we would deal with all the paperwork to come home later.

5th June 2001

Ro came early, collected me and took me home for breakfast and birthday hugs and kisses – although from a five-year-old's point of view... presents! Unfortunately, I started to feel quite poorly again and was experiencing more cramps, so I was glad to get through the next half-hour of smiles and 'Amy focus' to get back to hospital and lie down. Again, once I was resting everything subsided and I felt more comfortable. The baby's heartbeat was still healthy, so all was well. At about ten am I said to Ro that he might as well go to work. I expected to rest for a while longer before the hospital let me go home. "There's no point you just hanging around, love," I said. "You might as well get off and I'll ring you when they are letting me out."

At eleven am a nurse came in to check the monitor. The way she said, "Oh," when she looked at it made my heart sink. She hurriedly headed for the door with an, "I'll be right back."

"Is the baby okay?" I asked, panic racing through me.

"The heartbeat has just dipped a bit," she said, adding, "Don't worry I'll be right back."

She returned quite quickly with a doctor who looked at the monitor and said quite firmly, "We need to deliver this baby quickly. We'll take you down to delivery and check how dilated you are. If you are *not* about to give birth naturally, we'll have to do a Caesarean section."

Part of me was excited at the prospect of meeting my lovely little bundle earlier than expected and part of me was petrified that I would never get to meet my little bundle at all. As I was wheeled down the corridor the nurse told me she'd call Ro. Once we got in the delivery suite I was examined and, as I was only a couple of centimetres dilated, I was told that they would perform a Caesarean section. I was scared; I'd not had an operation before but trusted that this was the best thing for my baby. Because it was a rush it meant there was no time for an epidural so I had to be put to sleep. I was desperately longing for Ro to hold my hand and just to be there for our baby as it entered the world, given that *I* wouldn't be. Sadly, he didn't make it in time. Ro arrived shortly after our tiny little baby girl did, weighing in at 4lb 8ozs.

As my eyes blinked open there he was. "Hello darling! We have a beautiful little baby girl," he announced proudly. "I missed it by moments. She's doing great and they'll take you to see her soon. She's in the special care baby unit."

Relief flooded through me. Ahh, another little girl. We had previously been trying to decide between two names we both liked, Martha or Faith. "Let's call her Martha Faith," I suggested. Ro grinned, neither of us realising at that point just how appropriate her name would be.

Later that afternoon Ro wheeled me to the special care unit so that I could meet Martha. I was so excited to see her! She was a tiny little scrap all wired up in an incubator. And so cute. We got to hold her briefly, which was really special. I started to express breast milk, which was to be fed to her through the tube and then I would be able to breastfeed her once she was able to feed properly.

6th June 2001

I didn't feel great, but I put it down to having had an operation. As I hobbled down the corridor to see Martha my abdomen really hurt, it was hard to walk. As I arrived she was crying. I looked through the glass at the tiny little bundle that was our daughter; she appeared so tiny and fragile and I felt so useless. There was our dear little baby crying and there was nothing I could do to comfort her. I watched her for a moment, but then I couldn't stand it anymore. I hobbled back to my room, collapsed on the bed and sobbed.

My sisters Ruth and Alice (the former older by not quite two years, the latter younger by not quite five years) came to see me. It was a nice visit. They bought some really beautiful little clothes, looking like dolls' clothes. I could tell they had loved getting them.

When they left, Ruth gave me a huge hug. "Take care honey," she said. "I love you."

She much later told me this... Her and Alice had an argument in the car on the way home. Ruth said that she felt something was very wrong. Alice replied, "No, Martha's fine." To which Ruth had corrected, "It's Wendy, not Martha!" Alice told her she was being negative and they had a row about it. Ruth's senses were spot on! (She's always had a gift for picking things up).

8th June 2001

This day saw me feeling progressively worse. I didn't know what was happening. I hadn't been feeling great but had put it down to the Caesarean section. My previous two births had been natural and I'd never had a major operation before. Rather than easing in pain, however, my stomach had become more painful each day.

As the day drew on it grew so painful that I didn't know what to do with myself. I thought I had a chronic case of bad constipation.

I had been drinking peppermint tea and swallowed a number of laxatives in an attempt to alleviate the pain. They took me for an X-ray of my abdomen but couldn't see anything unusual. That night I just couldn't get comfortable, I tried lying and sitting but couldn't rest at all. The pain in my abdomen had become so intense I just wanted it to stop. It was really difficult to walk – as I struggled down the corridor to the toilet I had to hold the wall just to keep me upright, each step created searing pain.

I couldn't sleep at all as the pain was so constant. All I wanted was for the pain to stop!

9th June 2001

That night seemed to last an eternity. I was glad when the morning finally came and the nurse told me that a doctor from the ITU department was coming to take me over to the main hospital for an assessment. I didn't care what they did at that point; I just wanted the pain to go away. I can remember that it felt like an age before they were ready to move me. Various nurses and ambulance people and, I guess, doctors were busying around me, putting needles in my arms for drips and drugs. I was quite confused. It never crossed my logical mind that I might be dying. I thought that maybe I had appendicitis, they would give me a quick operation and I would be fine. I eventually travelled by ambulance to the main hospital and they took me into ITU. I didn't even know what ITU was; I now know it's the Intensive Therapy Unit, or Intensive Care for most of us.

The whole thing is very hazy; I can only remember that I thought they said I had meningitis. I was panicking that I had given it to my children and my sisters' children and they would all die. I had expressed some breast milk at the maternity hospital for Martha and I was very concerned that the Special Care Unit would feed it to her but that it was infected. "Ring the hospital to make sure they throw away the milk; don't give it to Martha!" I said to Ro. I do recall saying this quite a lot and apparently… I did. Ro and my Mum both came and had to wait. I don't remember seeing my Mum but I do remember seeing Ro. "Don't let them give Martha the milk" I repeated, probably about twenty times. Ro has since told me that I asked, "Will I be okay?" and I have no recollection of that. Then everything went black.

Chapter 2
Ro's Diary

12th June 2001

11:35 am

Today is the first day I feel strong enough to start this diary. Already I, and all your family have been through a rollercoaster ride of emotions; from disbelief, shock, and at times sheer terror, to relief and happiness.

A few days have passed so I had better wind back a bit and start this from the beginning.

Saturday morning I had a call from the maternity hospital saying that you would be transferred to the ITU department at Wonford. At that time, I believed this was purely for monitoring because your condition wasn't good and you'd had another bad night.

I arrived at the hospital just after twelve o'clock when Mum had arrived at the house to look after the kids. I sat in the waiting room for two hours, waiting to hear what was happening. Then a nurse led me in and let me see you. I'm not sure whether you remember this part, but you were awake and talking, and I was able to sit with you for a while.

A little later, your mum arrived and sat with both of us. Not long after that they had to sedate you because you were clearly distressed. Shortly before your sedation, Dr Purdey, one of the

ITU consultants, sat down with me and later with your mum, to start to try and explain why you were here.

It wasn't until I spoke with your mum later, that I truly appreciated how serious the situation was, but I'm jumping ahead a little here.

Dr Purdey took me into the interview room and explained that you were critically ill. I remember feeling completely numb as the shock set in. I couldn't feel anything and my mind went blank.

Dr Purdey then talked to your mum when she arrived and we were both allowed to come in and see you one more time before the sedation drugs took effect. I remember even then your concern was first for Katy, Amy and Martha. Before I go any further, let me put your mind at ease; as I write this Martha is doing really well. We are getting daily diary updates from the maternity hospital and Martha is now in the low dependency end of the ward. She's breathing normal air on her own and is taking milk through her feeding tube. The hope is that she'll be out of the incubator and into a normal cot in a few days.

So, as you were going under I hope I was able to let you know that the kids were fine. I also remember you looking at me and saying, "Am I going to be okay?" I really didn't know what to say.

It came home to me later when I spoke with your mum, just how seriously ill you were. We had both been sitting in the interview room, which has proven to be a quiet refuge from the main waiting room. While comparing what the consultant had said to us, it very much dawned on me that I could lose you. At that moment I felt such strong love for you that I knew no matter what, I was going to be there for you. I remember feeling despair at the possibility that you might not make it and that there was no way I would ever find anyone like you again. It was fate that brought us together and I'm damned well not going to lose you now. It's also strange that you said we should call Martha, Martha Faith. I've had to have faith that you are going to get better and she's been a kind of focus for me. Every day that I hear she's doing well it gives me strength to carry on. I need you Wendy, more than ever.

It's funny how people adopt stupid habits or beliefs, but I understand why now. It's a way of focusing your hope. They gave me your wedding ring on Sunday because your fingers were getting a bit puffy. I've taken to wearing it on my little finger, where I'm now determined it's going to stay until I can put it back on your finger myself. When I'm not in the room, it's a kind of link I have with you, and as long as it's on my finger I know you are going to be okay. I've also taken to looking at the cross in the chapel and saying a quiet, "Thank you," every time I pass. It's just something that happened.

So where am I? By this time, it's well into Saturday afternoon and they've taken you into theatre – they've established what is happening because your blood pressure is severely low. You've got a condition called Necrotising Fasciitis (NF). It's normally a fairly harmless bacteria, but in extremely rare cases it causes an erosion of the body's cells. This happens when the bacteria are killed and they release toxins into the body, which break it down.

That first period of surgery was the worst. Your condition was critical and without this surgery you were not going to survive. The surgery was successful and it also confirmed the diagnosis. The only option with NF is to remove the affected tissue; otherwise the dying cells cause those next to them to die. They have removed a lot of skin, principally from your stomach and up your sides to just below your armpits. Another consultant said that he estimated it to be the equivalent to a 40% burn. As well as skin they have had to take some muscle, to a greater or lesser degree, particularly over your stomach. Lastly, they've carried out a hysterectomy because it is from here that the bacteria started.

They aren't sure how the bacteria got into the wound, only that it obviously had. Once tissue becomes infected, there is no option other than to remove it. If any good news can be had, it's that once you've got the bacteria under control, they aren't going to come back. We are all just now hoping for several days of recovery.

During Saturday night they ran blood and fluids through you to keep you alive. It was quite shocking just how much was going in and leaking out again; there must have been at least 30 empty blood bags on the side at one time. Thankfully, your condition is now much more stable and the frantic activity of Saturday night is over, replaced by a much more sedate level of activity on Sunday and Monday.

On Saturday your mum stayed up all night. I was exhausted and went to bed about 11:15 pm. They have provided us with a room in the hospital so that we can be close at hand at all times. I think I've only been outside the hospital two or three times in the last three days. I woke at five am on Sunday morning to come down and find you in a stable condition. Your mum had managed to snatch an hour's sleep on the chair next door, but was clearly very tired, finally managing to get a couple of hours' sleep at about 6:30 am.

Sunday was much calmer, although we all realistically knew that your overall chances of survival were very much as they had been. The doctors did say, however, that you were much improved from the previous day. At ten am you went back into surgery to check that they had got all the infection. Apart from a very small area, the surgeons were happy they had got the worst of it although they stressed that in medicine there were no guarantees. The remainder of Sunday was quiet. I've seen so many doctors/consultants and nurses that I forget their names, but I know that each and every one has given you their absolute best care. I'll never be able to thank them enough, whatever the future holds.

I begin to lose track of time a little here, so I'll just write as I remember until we get to now, which is Tuesday 12th June at 3:50 pm.

There is one main drug, which is used to control your blood pressure, and it's called noradrenaline. Saturday you were on 40ml/hour, and it's been progressively lowering since. It is currently on (7) 14ml/hour. (It's a little confusing as they changed from single strength to double strength – you mentally have to double it to equate it to what you were given before, so it actually says 7).

Emotionally, I'm exhausted. For a couple of days if I thought that I might lose you, I'd break down. Over the last day, it's been getting easier, although we are all on a knife edge still, and will only really be happy when we know you are safe and stable. The doctors keep telling us that you have made a start on what will be a long road to recovery. I don't care how long that will take (other than how that affects you), because I'm here for you. There's no question that a part of me is in you and a part of you is in me. I'm not prepared to lose that bond, no matter what sacrifices we have to make. You've got me for life. It's as much about you needing me, as it is I needing you. Our family needs you. I have a very simple wish, which is nothing big to most people. Before I go to sleep I hope when I wake up you'll be just a little better. So far, we've been blessed that that's exactly what has happened.

Every time you've been into theatre the surgeons have come and spent time with us, both before and after. Thankfully, each time your condition is much better than they expected. It's funny what people take for granted, that they are fit and healthy and that their families are well, and for me, it's something I hope for.

The consultant plastic surgeon that is doing most of the surgery on you, showed us a couple of pictures of the extent of your injuries. Over the course of the last day or two, we'd become more and more positive, but these photos certainly slapped some home truths in our faces. He said it would help us to deal with it, and in turn help you, and he was right. We all had a low on Monday, still remembering the images of you that will be with us forever. Come Monday night, hope was renewed again when they completed another operation to cover your wound with skin that had been donated. We're told it is only a temporary covering because your body will reject it, but it gives you a chance to heal and get stronger. Only at that point can they replace the temporary skin with grafts from your own body.

I'm sure I've missed bits in catching up today, but I'll add them in when I remember. So here we are, Tuesday night and your heart rate is coming down. It's been around 122 for a day or two, then down to 110 and now 94 which is good news. Blood pressure has also improved, with less support from the drug noradrenaline. It's virtually back to normal, which is fantastic.

Took a break earlier and sat outside briefly, eating some lunch. Just as I got up, your ring slipped off my little finger and I spent the next couple of minutes looking for it in the grass. I really didn't need this! Suffice to say, I found it again quite quickly. For a moment I wondered if it was a sign of some kind. Finding it was such a welcome relief. As you already know, they gave me your ring on Sunday because your fingers were swelling up and they didn't want to have to cut it off.

Remembered some extra things from yesterday. A young autistic girl was admitted to the unit and as she was waking up, she sounded extremely distressed. At first it sounded like someone writhing in agony. This morning she was still going, but much better than she was. Since then she has been put on a ward.

11:35 pm

Just come back to the room to get a few hours' sleep. Just before I left the nurse was cleaning your mouth and you seemed to become much more awake. I'm sure you could hear what we were saying to you, although whether you remember or not I don't know. I told you that we (your mum and I) were here for you and that all the kids were fine.

You seemed so rested today, your face looked really beautiful and I still can't believe that I have had the wonderful opportunity to be with you.

The plastic surgeon said the other day that the skin grafts on your body were going to look awful for a long time, but also that you would be amazed by what your body can do.

I've always thought of you as the prettiest woman I've known, and his words confirmed for me the feeling that I have inside. It's not about how you look on the outside; it's that spark behind your eyes, and the warmth in your smile that I fell in love with. That feeling is stronger than it has ever been.

I know it's going to be hard for you to have to deal with everything that's happened to you; even today, the consultant said that as a side effect of your overall condition it was likely that you would lose a couple of toes from each foot. Wendy: You have to see past that superficial beauty and focus on who you are – an amazing and, in every sense of the word, beautiful woman who is loved by all your family and with whom my life has a purpose.

Good night sweetheart, and I will see you bright and early tomorrow.

Wednesday 13th June

6:10 pm

Another eventful day. Woke this morning much more refreshed, and came down at around nine am. Another stable night with some of the drugs turned down, which was a good sign. However, today's big story is really how well you are recovering. During the course of this morning, they've completely stopped the noradrenaline, which was supporting your blood pressure. This, for me was a major milestone. You've also started to take in food, which is another good sign. Kidneys too, are kick-starting again, which points to your getting better all the time.

Today you've been the most active you've been so far. In the last few days you were lying pretty still, but now you're moving your head and your face is much more expressive.

The plastic surgeon has looked at your skin today, and is happy that everything is going as expected. The plan for the next day is to put some foam-filled gadget over your wound. This is used to suck out toxins and promote blood flow, which is there primarily to support the temporary skin.

I can't remember if I talked to you about your toes before. Yesterday the ITU consultant said – and I reiterate – that you would probably lose a couple of toes from each foot as an effect of the septicemia. Today, however, the news was very different. It looks much more likely that your toes will be more intact than they anticipated, so they are just going to wait a few days to see how things go.

Today's star sign was amazingly appropriate for you! So much so that we have cut it out and stuck it on your wall, together with the growing number of pictures and cards. It basically said that today you'd achieve more than you thought you could, and you sure have! I won't repeat the words; you can read them for yourself.

Looking slightly longer term, the plan now is for you to stay in ITU for a couple of weeks to allow your strength to continue to grow. Not until then can they start to graft skin onto your sides. Your tummy area which was the worst affected will be completed last as they know the longer they leave it, the better chance of successful surgery.

I left the hospital grounds today for the first time since Saturday to visit the maternity hospital and see Martha. No amount of daily photos can compare to just a minute with her. I enjoyed a big cuddle with lots of smiles and wriggles. Ruth arrived with the kids and I had a really nice hug with Katy and Amy who were really sweet. Of course, they both got a cuddle too which they thoroughly enjoyed. The girls are now residing at their father's for a little bit whilst we make plans for the longer term.

Rachie Love, who has been with Ruth for a few days, came down to see you. She's so bubbly (and was perhaps a bit too much for me today), but it was nice to see her. I know that she'd give anything to see you get better, so a bit of extra noise was a small price to pay.

Well it's creeping towards seven pm now, and I'm just starting to get hungry. I'm hoping the canteen has as delicious a supper as last night (kofta curry).

11:11pm

Supper turned out to be Italian meatballs and spaghetti. I was fairly convinced the meatballs were the leftovers from the kofta curry the previous evening, but it tasted nice so I didn't really care. Besides, I was hungry.

At about nine pm, Ginnette phoned the unit and we chatted. Without going into too much detail I condensed the last five days into a couple of minutes. I felt it best that she knew how serious the situation was. By the end she was crying down the phone. After that conversation with Ginnette I was asked by Gwill, who had come down again that evening, whether I was okay. The last five days have undoubtedly been very difficult indeed, but today the improvements you've made have given us renewed hope. We are confident that you will continue to make good progress. From Ginnette's viewpoint, things must have seemed very different, as she obviously hadn't prepared herself mentally for what I was about to tell her. So, yeah, I was fine (relatively speaking), but poor Ginnette will have that same journey as the rest of us before she starts to come to terms with what has happened.

Rachie Love and Ruth left earlier, and I've spent a lot of the time talking to Alice and giving her some of the background on my wayward family. It passed the time and she seemed happy enough to listen. This whole episode has drawn both families very close together – it's now more like having one big family. Your sisters especially, have shown a strength and compassion I would otherwise have never seen. Each day that passes they feel more like my sisters too. Your mum has been a diamond too. Her relentless faith in you has been resolute from the start as she determinedly sits with Alice and I during the seemingly long days. As a mother, I cannot even begin to imagine the strength she must have to be here. But then I think, she herself is drawing from the amazing resilience and will for life that *you* have, and in turn radiates out to all of us. I pray once again for a stable and safe night and I will see you again in the morning. One last thing before I say goodnight – we've been occasionally listening to the radio whilst sitting in with you, and yesterday I heard the lyrics to the new Faithless song. The words were so appropriate, they could have been written for us. The track is entitled 'We Come One' and the lyrics say so much about how I feel about you. I love you, Wendy Gilhespy.

Thursday 14th June

2:00 pm

With much relief, I came down this morning to find that you'd had another good night. They had to increase your ventilation a little, but nothing in particular to worry about. Your kidneys continue to improve and they hope you will be off the filtration machine in the next day or two. Everything else is much the same as the day before. Your blood pressure and heart rate remain good and you're continuing to take food, which is a great sign. Periodically, the nurses have to suck fluid up from your stomach to see how well you are absorbing it. That, and squeezing it back in again, is one of the top worst bits of their jobs.

The plan today is much the same as yesterday: do nothing. Your hands and arms have been in slings to ease the fluid in your hands and they've also been able to bring them down today.

We spoke with Alistair, the ITU consultant again and he confirmed that your condition was getting much better. This was tempered with the realisation that your condition would be potentially life threatening for the next few months, until all the wounds are covered in your own skin again. We are all still treading on such an emotional tightrope, that as different things improve or decline, it has been mirrored in all our moods. Considering the stress we have all been under, we've been doing amazingly well together – especially considering that your mum and I have been sharing a tiny room together for the past five nights.

Tomorrow afternoon the plan is to put a special gadget over your wound; this will promote the blood flow and draw toxins away from the tissue. It will probably stay on until Tuesday morning, but as with all these things, it's flexible.

One thing I didn't mention earlier – Alistair mentioned that many people thought you might not have made it over the weekend. The fact you're still here, improving all the time is, as one guy here said, a miracle. Thank god for miracles.

11:55 pm

A quiet end to the day. You were stable throughout and continually improve. The plan for tomorrow is to remove you from the filtration machine to see how your kidneys cope independently. Hopefully it will be another milestone and yet further improvement in your overall health.

We were all joking today at how everyone is taking an active interest in how much you are peeing. Medically it's a good sign that your kidneys are working again, but on its own it does sound rather odd. "Come on Wendy, pee some more!" On that note my dearest Schmoo, I will say goodnight.

Friday 15th June

7:35 pm

I always wonder whether there is going to be much to write; will it just be a 'more of the same' day? I've come to realise that there aren't going to be many 'same old day's for some time to come.

I've retreated to the quiet of the hospital room, having just had another surprisingly good meal in the canteen. I find myself much more aware of my own mortality, and mentally pat myself on the head when I've finished my fresh orange juice. It helps me through the day.

Spirits are generally high. Your condition continues to be very stable, and we've reached a couple more milestones. Just so that you can say you've had one too, today they did a tracheostomy, which will allow them to reduce the sedatives that you are on. This you continue to fight, in typical Wendy style, wanting to wake up. It will also let them administer drugs more easily and will prove to be far more comfortable for you.

The pressure dressing is now on your wound, sucking out the toxins and doing its stuff. The plan is for this to stay on until Tuesday before reviewing it again after that. The other biggie is that they have turned off the filtration machine in the wake of your kidneys coming back on line. At this point it's not clear how well they are working, so it's likely you may need to go back on the machine for a while whilst your vital organs continue to improve.

They will know tomorrow just how functional your kidneys are right now, when the blood tests come back.

Ginnette phoned again and I let her know how everything was going. She seemed much more positive and very pleased with the improvements you'd made. I even made her laugh; a very different conversation to the one we'd shared before.

Ruth came down again and took turns sitting in with me, your mum and Alice, although we all had some time away because of the things they needed to do.

I didn't mention that they have now burst the blisters on your lower legs and feet, and covered your legs with dressings. It's been mentioned that taking a few photos would help you whilst you recover, to see how bad you were, and just how far you've come. I'm all for that, but it's measured with some concern that the whole thing will dehumanise what's happening.

Alice wanted to take another picture of your feet. Rightly or wrongly it just made me feel it was all very clinical. I don't want us to go over the top with it.

Early afternoon I went to see Martha, who continues to do extremely well. They are all pleased with her progress and are now starting one hour feeds, rather than continuously, as they have been. She's wearing the clothes Alice bought her. Your sisters have taken your mum to Mothercare who once again bought most of it! I think they've been planning to get us out of the hospital once in a while so I chatted with Ruth about this later. She was concerned that your mum, and I also, would eventually have to deal with it but I don't think for me, at least, now is the right time. I'm not leaving the hospital for some time until I know you are much better. I'm aware I am not going to be here for six months, as you may be, but it's too early to think about going home yet.

Phoned work this morning and briefly explained what had happened. They were extremely good about it and have basically given me as long as I like which takes the pressure off. Well, it's eight pm so I'm going back down to sit with you a while longer. I may even try and read a little of the Red Dwarf books Brian brought in.

11:05 pm

No luck with the Red Dwarf books, just not in any particular mood to read. Just left your mum foot-tapping to S Club 7 and other classic tunes on Gemini FM. It's become a bit of a routine over the last two or three nights.

Ruth and Alice left to see Jayne and Paul earlier. Apparently Jayne has completely been in pieces since she heard what had happened.

Depending on the results of your blood tests tomorrow, you may or may not need to go back on the filtration machine. I'm hoping you won't need it, but it's in no way a setback if you do. I just have to keep reminding myself of this fact.

Despite me saying earlier that I thought it was too early for Ruth to be talking about us being away from the hospital, I now think she was probably right. At least in the sense that just by mentioning it, it has started me thinking about when that may be.

I also think that for your mum, it's more of a case of Ruth and Alice guiding her in the right direction, which I agree she needs. I will do my usual visit to Martha again tomorrow, and record here how it went. I pray again for a stable and safe night. Goodnight sweetheart.

Saturday 16th June

8:25 pm

Medically, a quiet day. Our game of 'Measure the Pee' continues, and your kidneys seem to be really coming on strong. It now looks likely that you won't need to go back on the filtration machine, which is excellent. The other thing that happened today was that your ventilation has been altered so that you can now breathe for yourself – it's there if it's needed. Your oxygen is now at 39%, which is the lowest it's been and is again, really good – 21% and you're breathing normal air.

Your friend Jon came in today, which for me was rather odd as I always saw him as one of Andy's mates. He was pleasant enough but we didn't really talk that much.

Alice and Ruth left just after five to see Katy and Amy and make sure they are both okay. I'll hear how they are tomorrow on their return.

I visited Martha again. She was sleeping in her cot so I didn't want to wake her, as she looked so peaceful.

There was a strange sense of irony about the whole situation; both of you in ITU, both looking so peaceful and both with a feeding tube up your noses – very strange.

The doctors discussed your toes again. A couple of them on both feet look pretty black at the ends and it's a fair bet the tips will be removed. It's a very minor operation but they don't anticipate doing it for a few months.

For me, today has been a day of reflection. The whole event very much makes you aware of your own mortality, and the fragility of life. One of the nurses, Tara I think, was saying how the slightest thing in your body could cause big things to go wrong. Equally, I said how remarkable your body is, and you are living proof of that.

Around lunchtime I wandered outside for a while, and sat on a bench that I'd used several times before. I noticed an inscription on it, 'In memory of Joan Ward' and it made me wonder who this lady was, and just how many people had sat there.

The plan for tomorrow, or possibly Monday, is to slowly reduce the sedatives and bring you round. For most of today I've actually felt excited about the prospect of being able to speak to you again, after a week in the wilderness. However, I'm starting to feel a little concerned because I'm not sure what your state of mind will be. There's going to be a lot to tell and I have no idea how well you'll hold together. What is important is that I'm there for you.

The doctors also added that the tracheostomy could cause some people distress because they can't speak.

Mum came in again this evening. She tends to go over to see Martha later in the day, around feeding time. She tried Martha on a bottle and she took 10ml of it. Considering her hourly intake is 16ml, which was pretty good going. The midwives are continuing with the diary and additional video footage has been taken. Everyone over there has been really brilliant.

It's been a day of everyone telling me how well I am doing. I'm holding together pretty well, but other than that, I'm only doing what anyone else would do. The reassurance is nice but it does make me wonder what it's all for.

10:55 pm

The end of another remarkable day. Something changed today, that 'what if?' has changed into 'when you're better!' My faith that you're going to get better has got stronger. It's always been there, but I've found myself previously tempering good news with the 'what ifs'. Ruth said today that she had 'sensed' something was wrong before this all started, like when the cat died, and her first husband was in hospital. Ruth now says that that feeling has gone from her. Let's all pray we're right. See you tomorrow.

Sunday 17th June

11:07 pm

I've not had a chance to write anything until now. The sedation has been turned off on one of the drugs they were giving you, and today, for the first time in a week, I was able to talk to you again. I took heart from the occasional smiles and squeezes of my hand,

and the small signs of affection with you stroking the side of my face.

So far, things have gone pretty well. You're still pretty groggy, but you've coped amazingly well. The tracheostomy tube was very uncomfortable at first, but this seemed to settle down later in the day. The problem with having the tube in is that you can't cough properly. The irritation doesn't go away unless the nurses use a special tube by sliding it inside the main tube – judging by the expression on your face, it's not a particularly pleasant experience.

You have been drifting in and out of sleep a lot, regularly shaking your head. I can only presume you are dreaming, or perhaps a half dream, and can't really believe where you are.

It seems that the trauma of the last week has blanked out your recollection of how you got to the ITU. I'm not sure if that memory will return but today you had no recollection of arriving in the ambulance.

It was nice to show you pictures of Martha, and give you updates on her progress. Lots of smiles were received from you whenever her name was mentioned.

One other thing you've done a lot of is drifting off to sleep, only to wake with a start. This continued repeatedly during the day before seeming more settled tonight. You've also woken up and stared at your hands, fallen asleep again, only to do it moments later. I think the low level of sedatives you are taking is making it difficult for you to stay awake for long and it also impairs your memory. I have a feeling that you will have a much stronger recollection after the event.

Your mum went back to our house at ten pm today, the first night she has slept away from the hospital. I'm not sure how much of it is her idea and how much Ruth and Alice's. Maybe it's what your mum needs anyway, so I guess it doesn't matter.

Speaking of Ruth and Alice, they visited again and were really chuffed to see you awake. They'll be back down again on Tuesday. I think for all of us, today was an opportunity to say things to you that we didn't have a chance to when you were first brought in. For me, to look into your eyes again, and see Wendy staring back at me, was everything. Sleep well my love.

Monday 18th June

12:15 pm

Just popped back to the room to jot down some thoughts while they change your bedding.

I had a very weird dream of you last night of being much better and standing beside the bed. I remember being concerned that you had gotten out of bed but you seemed perfectly happy. From the front, you just looked like you had a few long stitches that had pretty much healed, but then you turned sideways and the area under your ribs and all the way down to your pelvis, was extremely thin. I panicked, thinking you might snap in half and I urged you to lie down again. That's all I remember.

Mum has left to see Martha now, and will no doubt come back with an update of her progress. I'm coming back down to see you again, as you made it quite clear you didn't like me leaving you alone in the room.

10:15 pm

I'm exhausted. Today has been the hardest so far. It's only 10:15 and I feel completely drained. Thankfully, you drifted off to sleep and let me get away to some much-needed catch-up sleep.

It's beginning to dawn on me now just what a long and difficult road lies ahead, and what strength and courage you will need along the way. I feel that each moment I sit with you and hold your hand, a little bit of my strength goes into you. I'm deeply touched by the love you so clearly have for me – obvious even through the haze of sedatives and sheer exhaustion. Several times today you've needed me to be there and did not want me to leave. I will always be there for you Wendy, and if each day drains me completely, it doesn't matter because we will get through this together. The love you give to me inspires hope and joy, and forever reminds me of just what a wonderful woman you are.

It's been distressing seeing you clearly in some discomfort because of the tracheostomy tube. I sincerely hope that in some small way I have been able to comfort you. It was really nice to watch you drift off into a peaceful sleep and I hope you wake tomorrow that little bit stronger. Now *I* need sleep. Goodnight sweetheart.

Tuesday 19th June

12:20 pm

I try to leave you for as little as I can each day. It's tiring but it's worth it. I've been feeling a bit flat looking towards that long road ahead and the journey we must take. However, whenever I think of the difficulties, both emotionally and physically that we must endure, I realise how easy my part will be compared with the strength that I know you have that *you* will need to get through this.

This was also the first day the doctors pretty much spelt out what had happened to you, and they didn't leave a lot out. The choice was either to operate on you or you were going to die, it's that simple.

Whilst you may have heard everything that was said, I sincerely doubt that the sheer scale of what you've come through, and what you have yet to face has truly dawned on you.

Right now they're changing the pressure bandage, giving you a good clean and a change of bedding. You still looked uncomfortable on the trachy tube again this morning, but thank goodness it was better than the previous day.

What I'm hoping for is that the dressing has done its job and is working properly. When they are done, no doubt we'll have another chat. The plastic surgeon, Mr Inglefield, said that it could be anywhere between two to four weeks before the temporary skin is rejected by your body and then your own skin is used to replace it. Until then, we're in a kind of limbo, waiting each day for you to get stronger.

2:10 pm

Everything seems to be okay. The dressings are doing their job. Two problems discovered during the dressing change are that you have a hole in your bowel (which could be serious) and some of the tissue on one thigh may need to be removed. They aren't going to do anything about either yet and will, in the meantime, just continue to let you get stronger.

It has also been a day of isolated twinges of panic; I don't know what I'd do without you and I know that we are a long way from getting you home. I begin to wonder whether the others are now expecting you to pull through, rather than just hoping.

11:45 pm

Much more of the Wendy I knew came out. The odd smile, your hand brushed against my face and something bright in your eyes. If I were to judge how well you were doing, today would be the best on that alone.

In reality it was a very mixed day. You nearly managed to get your feeding tube out and later on you started picking at one of your bandages, which for me, was a good sign.

The morning was pretty tiring for you with the dressing change on your stomach and legs. You were very unsettled for much of the morning but increasingly better after a good sleep. I found I had renewed energy around seven pm, which is one of the reasons I didn't leave until nearly midnight. The day, which was hard to start, was much easier than I had expected. I've managed to read a fair part of a Red Dwarf book. It helps pass long hours whilst you sleep and I can still be there beside you. It does feel a bit strange sometimes, looking up from my book, to find myself still sitting in ITU.

It has also been tinged with some concern. Whilst the dressing and temporary skin looked good, there were some setbacks. During the dressing change they found a hole in your bowel and some tissue near your thigh, which may need surgery; I think I mentioned that earlier.

Most importantly, I found Wendy again and it made the long day so much easier.

Wednesday 20th June

10:45 pm

Another good day. Wendy returned in force, first putting two fingers up to Ruth and then calling me a doughnut! (Well, writing it). It was writing day. After a somewhat shaky start, Wend quickly got the hang of it again and we managed to communicate quite a lot. That, together with several facial expressions and gestures, it was starting to get easier to understand what Wendy wanted; namely having her teeth brushed, three times!

It was during one of the teeth brushing sessions that the doughnut remark was made. There I was, getting Wend to rinse out her mouth and spit it into a paper towel, when sitting next to me was the suction tube I'd seen them use a hundred times before. Doughnut!

It was also another rest day – very little in the way of change, although we did have one little step forward. Wend was put on a tracheostomy mask, which means she could still get a good supply of oxygen, but she would be doing it all herself. At the moment the ventilator she is on lets her breathe herself, but gives a little extra boost after each breath.

Wend stayed on the mask on two separate occasions, totalling just over an hour. The hope is to lose the ventilator completely over the next couple of days.

The big event of today was undoubtedly the arrival of Martha. Wendy was dead tired but there was no doubt she enjoyed seeing her for the first time in over a week. They took a couple of photos, one for the diary and another for us to keep here.

In the coming weeks the hope is to have Martha over here on Bramble ward, so that Wendy can see her more easily.

You'll excuse me if I flit between 'you' and 'Wendy'. It all depends on when I get to write the diary and how tired I am.

Tomorrow, Ruth, Alice (who were here again today) and Rachie Love, will be down to see you. I'm concerned they'll tire you out too much but I know that's just my irrational fear poking through.

I have to say that it was also a day of smiles. Your sisters got some good ones out of you and I see you've made an ally with one of the nurses, Tara, who we all agree is an absolute star and would win Big Brother if she were to enter. On a more serious note, it does make me realise how important it is for some kind of bond between nurse and patient, so that you trust all the nurses will do their very best for you. There is no doubt that Tara is your favourite.

Digging deeper into the Red Dwarf book, I've come across the part about 'better than life'. Sometimes I wonder if we're in that game and we don't know it, only it's 'worse than life'.

Each day gets a little easier and the time passes a little faster. I keep reminding myself that for each day you are in that bed, it's a day less you'll be in it.

Chapter 3
Back to Life

Where was I during the period of sedation?

The following are the various dreams/memories that I recall from that time:

I am on holiday with another couple and we are going to work in a bar. We all get very drunk and end up having a threesome when we get back to the hotel. I don't want to but I am paralysed; they use me and there is nothing I can do about it. Finally they stop, leave me alone and the nightmare is over. I cry myself to sleep.

Another is that I am on a long plane flight. I am returning from Australia and I am pregnant. I am worrying because Ro might think it is not his baby but I know that it is.

I think I'm at a train station. It's a big, old building with high atrium ceilings and loads of gorgeous light is flooding in. Suddenly there is lots of commotion and a man has been shot in the stomach. There is blood everywhere, at which point I suddenly realise it is me. *I* have been shot in the stomach, am bleeding like crazy and the pain is horrendous. People are all around me and they are going to take me to the hospital.

I am flitting between two places. Firstly, I am on an alien ship. It is fairly small and there are some stairs off to my left. I am lying on a bed on my back and I cannot move. Six, pink aliens are moving around me. They are what I would call classic alien shape, with large heads and floaty limbs. They seem to drift around me and they are chatting, but I don't know what they are saying. They come nearer, two either side of the bed. They are rolling me and ow! it hurts. Pain sears down my sides. 'Please leave me alone,' I think, but I can't speak. 'No, don't move me, just leave me. Who are you? Where am I? I am ill and I am in the wrong hospital. How did I get here?' They roll me again, and then I hear a voice, a pleasant happy voice saying, "Just a bit of cold spray on your bottom, my love." I feel a cold sensation and then I am rolled back over onto my back. I am still, I relax, and everything goes black.

I am now in a small room, in what looks like an ordinary hospital. It is quite bright and Ro is holding my hand. I feel relief, ahh there he is... he makes me feel safe. There is a curtain to my left with a sort of checked pattern on it. On the wall in front of me I see a round thing; I'm not sure, but I think it is a clock. To the left of the clock are tiny little boxes – what's that inside them? It looks like baby booties. A baby, I think I have a tiny baby. I'm not sure though. Where is it? I remember it is a girl and she is in hospital, but this is not the room I was in. Why am I here? It all feels very strange and dreamlike, however, I feel safe because Ro is holding my hand.

I'm back in the space ship. Where is Ro? I panic. What are they doing now? 'Stop! Yuck, that's horrible.' They are blowing smoke into my lungs. 'Oh my god,' I think. 'I am NEVER going to smoke again, it's disgusting!' Ro will be pleased, he always hated me smoking. Oh no… they are coming close again, they are going to roll me again. 'Please leave me alone, don't touch me,' I silently plead. I drift into darkness.

I am in the ordinary room again and, joy, Ro is there and holding my hand. He is talking to someone across the bed. I am unaware whom. There is a door to my left behind the checked curtain. A couple of men come in. It's Henry Kelly and some other celebrity. 'Where have I seen him?' I remember it is the chap with the beard who was the PE instructor in Grange Hill in the 1980s. 'I wonder why they are here. This is still the wrong room. I must get back to the hospital I am supposed to be in.'

I'm back on the space ship. 'Oh no, I don't want to be here. I'm scared.' I'm drifting around the space ship and up near the roof is a wooden cast (like they have on the front of a boat) of Jesus' face. If only I could get out of here; maybe I can will the bed backwards. I try with all my might to will the bed out of the wall behind me... I concentrate really hard… nothing. I am exhausted and I drift into darkness.

I'm back in the ordinary room. Where is Ro? He's gone. I need him. I reach out with my right hand. He'll be back in a minute. He has got something that will make me better. I reach and reach, 'Come on Ro, I need you. Hurry up!' I keep reaching and I keep waiting. It feels like I have been waiting for ages. I feel angry! I slam my hand down on the bed. 'Stuff you then!' The brief burst of anger is very quickly replaced by fear. 'Please come back, I need you'… I drift into darkness yet again.

I'm still in the ordinary room and I know that Ro has my wedding ring as it is on his watch. Good, it is safe but he has left it all on the window ledge. A man is stealing it and I am powerless to do anything. 'How silly to leave it there.' I am cross. Now it is gone forever. I drift off. Ro is here now and I try to tell him I'm in the wrong hospital, but I cannot speak. I try to gesture for him to push my bed out of the window, then I can escape and I will find my way back to the right hospital. My niece is on the window ledge. What the hell is she doing? She's only fifteen. It's late, it's dark. She is with her boyfriend and they have come down on his motorbike. Ruth will be worried sick. I'm trying to tell Ro but I cannot speak. How frustrating. Eventually, after much gesturing, I manage to get Ro to understand. Ro goes to them and he will take them back to our house. My mum is staying there and she can ring my sister who will duly sort them out in the morning. Relief... panic over. Days pass and I don't see Ro. I hear that he has had a motorbike accident. He took my niece's boyfriend's bike and had a crash, the idiot. He has really smashed up his face; oh my god, that's all I need. But he is back very rapidly because he has used BUPA and they fixed him up really quickly.

Near death

I am floating while being surrounded by a sea of light. The forward gliding motion is beautifully effortless and I am unaware of my physical body, but still aware of 'me'. I exist, which surprises me as I am not my body. I am totally enraptured by the overwhelming sense of peace. No words could ever do it justice. It is so utterly delicious, like no experience on earth – a heavenly peace. I have no thoughts of anything other than continuing to ride the wave of peace that carries me forwards. The light is overwhelmingly beautiful and all around me but brighter and ahead of me. I want to keep going into it; I am quite happy to be taken wherever this flow is carrying me.

I look ahead and see the outline of silhouettes beginning to reveal themselves by taking shape in the far distance. I cannot make them out clearly. Suddenly I feel a massive tug on my arm and I come to an abrupt halt. I glance behind me and see that I am holding Ro's hand, which is making me stop.

I pull hard on his hand because I really want to keep going into this glorious all-encompassing peace and light. There is no movement. It is so very inviting and I have no thoughts other than to keep moving towards the light. We will go together, I think. I pull harder on his hand but he does not budge. It is then that I hear the voice in my mind. I know that it is coming from the forms ahead of me saying, "If you come, you must come on your own." Looking back at Ro once more I feel an overwhelming urge to carry on floating into this amazing serenity. I really want him to come with me, and without a second thought, I pull hard on his hand. However, it is like he is stuck fast in concrete and he doesn't move an inch. My desire to go further into the exquisite light is still all-encompassing and yet I do not want to leave him behind.

I look forward towards the forms imploringly, and again, am met with the same words in my mind, "If you come, you must come on your own." Knowing that my efforts to bring him with me are futile I release my forward intentions and finally stop. The overpowering urge to continue subsides and is replaced with the knowledge that I must make a choice. It's an easy one – I choose to be wherever he is. There is no need to communicate this to the sea of light or the forms because it/they already know my choice. Then gently, the experience fades.

****

My mum's friend Tricia is in the doorway. She is wearing yellow and black. "I can't stop long," she says, "It's family only but I so wanted to see you." She's gone. Ro is still there and he is holding my hand. I hear a loud 'BANG!' and I hear someone exclaim, "Don't worry, the emergency generator will kick in in a minute." A plumber comes to fix the sink because it is leaking. He doesn't have the right tools and needs to come back again.

On the 17th June they reduced the sedation and woke me up. The dreams were a strange mix of reality and fantasy. In the initial days Ro and Mum held my hand constantly. I wonder if I would have gone if they had not done this because there would have been nothing to anchor me here. I do remember dreaming a great deal that Ro was gone, and I was banging my hand on the bed for him to hold it. Apparently, I actually did this. I think the sense of being in the wrong hospital was because the maternity unit was a separate site back then, and I had been moved to the main hospital away from Martha. I obviously knew this on some level. My mum's friend Tricia really did pop her head round the door wearing black and yellow; the bang *was* the generator; the plumber *did* come and go again to get more tools and one of the nurses *did* look like Henry Kelly!

Waking up!

17th June

Ro's face was looking at me. He looked tired and drained. Feelings of confusion washed over me. 'What's going on?' I thought. 'Where am I?' A soft smile spread over his face, "Hello Wend," he said. "It's good to see you." I went to speak but couldn't. What was happening? Where was I? "You're in hospital," he explained. "You were poorly after having Martha. Do you remember?"

Martha: the name swam into my head. Yes I remembered, our tiny little baby girl who was premature and in the incubator. He must have seen the concern flash across my face. "She's doing great," he reassured me. Again, that soft smile and a flash of relief blinked across his face. I could feel the warmth of his hand but I couldn't move. Suddenly I was aware that my mum was there too. "Hello darling," she said, the brave face trying to hide the tears in her eyes.

"Hi Wendy, I'm Tara," said a cheerful, friendly-looking nurse, "Are you in any pain? I can give you more pain relief. If you need it just blink your eyes." I was in intense pain, not physically right in that moment but a sense of despair and confusion that I couldn't bear and just wanted to escape from. I blinked and she pressed a button to administer more morphine. I instantly felt a sense of ease spread through me. It eased a little, but I was still in turmoil. I blinked again and she administered a little more. This time I closed my eyes and drifted off to sleep.

The second time of waking was easier than the first. As the room swam into view I wondered what those babies' booties were doing on the wall of an intensive care hospital ward. Ro and Mum were still there. "Hello," they both said in unison. I could see the relief on their faces. This time I knew that I was in hospital, but I had no idea what had gone on or how long I had been there. It was so lovely to see Ro, I felt safe while he was holding my hand. He must have seen the confusion on my face and so, for the second time, told me what had happened. "You have been very poorly. You are so strong," he said, his voice faltering a little, "and you are going to be fine. You can't speak at the moment because of the ventilator; it's helping you to breathe right now." Yuck! That was what that strange feeling in my throat was. It felt really uncomfortable.

This repeated pattern of waking in confusion continued throughout the rest of the day. My family told me afterwards that one of them would tell me a little of what had happened. Then they would have to leave the room to dissolve in their own despair while the other one stayed behind, chatting and holding my hand; each time thinking that would be it, yet only to be faced by the same confusion from me time and again.

I began to regain some movement and gesture for things – the morphine dose changed from me having to blink to making an upward gesture with the fingers from an upturned hand. I remember on several occasions gesturing more and more as I just wanted to go to oblivion and escape from where I was.

19th June

The surgeon came, introduced himself and proceeded to tell me what had happened. He told me everything that they had done, not leaving anything out. The severity of what had happened and the fragility of my health were beyond my comprehension. It simply didn't register. Instead I had two thoughts: Firstly I wanted to ask if I could take a quick shower, and secondly I wondered if I could just pop home and get some things for the baby. Then my head began to swim in a total fog of utter confusion. I couldn't even think. I was so tired; it was really hard to keep my eyes open. As my eyes closed, sleep took me again.

The dressings have been changed. They took me to theatre to do this while I was sedated, but afterwards it was really painful. I wish they'd leave me alone but I know they can't, obviously.

20th June

Today's big change is coming off the ventilator and beginning to breathe for myself again. In order to do this, the doctors have given me a tracheostomy mask. This means that they remove me from being connected to the ventilator and put a mask on me instead. It delivers a high content of oxygen. Who would have thought that breathing could be so exhausting! The first attempt was really hard, made worse by feeling really afraid. I was worried that I would not be able to get enough air. The first attempt lasted for about ten minutes, mostly with me being focused on it being over and imagining the relief of being put back on the ventilator. The second attempt went much better; it wasn't quite such a labour and I think I relaxed much more which made breathing easier. It was hard work though, and I was relieved when it was over so I could get back on the ventilator, and drift off to sleep.

It's also been a day of visitors. I've seen Ruth, Alice and Martha.

It was lovely to see them. Ruth and I have always been very close. One of the things I have always loved about Ruth is her fantastic sense of humour and quick wit. Even in the midst of these devastating circumstances it was still there.

From when I was about eight I remember feeling fat. Although when I look back at photos I'm a bit plump, but not fat. I used to stand with my back arched and my stomach sticking out which obviously didn't help! At age eleven I had size eight feet and was about the height I am now (5'7"). My big feet were a real cause for heartache as shoes in size seven and eight were uncommon when I was eleven. Now it's really common, but back then I felt like a freak. I was pleased with my height but had always wanted to be thinner (especially to have slimmer thighs) and to weigh less.

As Ruth walked into the room her opening comment to me was, "Well… they could have taken a bit off your thighs while they were at it!" Mum's reaction was shock, spluttering, "You can't say that!" I loved it though. It made me laugh inside so much; a mighty fine tonic. Humour and laughter is very healing. It's not always easy to find the rays of entertainment when you are in your darkest hours, but it's definitely one of the best things you can try and do.

It was wonderful to see Ruth. She had looked after Katy and Amy for the first few days before they went to stay with their dad. She filled me in on how they were and had some funny stories about them. Grace (Ruth's daughter) and Katy had dressed up as boys and gone over to the park. They were called Bubbles and Adam and they had even played football with some other boys. It was so good to hear that the girls were okay. Ruth also told me that her and one of my oldest friends Rachel, had come in to see me while I was sedated. Rachel had said, "What do we do?" to which Ruth had replied, "I think she can hear us, so let's just chat to her and tell her what we've been doing." Rachel and Ruth can both be quite loud, and as they were chatting away to me and laughing together, I started getting restless and trying to come round from the sedation. So much so, that the nurse asked them to leave. This really made me chuckle... the idea of them being chucked out of intensive care for being too rowdy!

I'm so physically weak that gesturing has been exhausting in the attempt to communicate what I want. I wanted my glasses so that

I could see clearly. I'm very short-sighted. Given my hazy thought process I don't always follow the most logical route. When I wanted my glasses, instead of putting circles with my fingers to my eyes or something more obvious, instead I just pointed at Ro because *he* wears glasses. It was very frustrating when Mum, Ro, Ruth and Alice couldn't work out what I wanted. Finally, bless them, they got what I meant. As the glasses were placed over my eyes, I could finally see what those boxes of babies' booties were. They weren't boxes or babies' booties at all, they were photographs. Photographs of the kids, of our family and me. Initially it was a nice reminder of normality, but then they made me feel sad. It made me miss Katy and Amy even more and the special time that we should now all be sharing with our newest family member.

Thank heavens for morphine at those moments when suddenly, psychologically, emotionally, mentally or physically it was just too painful. I retreated into the bliss of the escapism that the drugs brought, prior to slipping into a deep sleep. Unfortunately, escaping into oblivion did not change the circumstances, and on waking I was repeatedly faced with the same horror story that was of me with a mutilated body, lying in a hospital bed. If I was alive there was no other way around this than to face it. Gradually today, the severity of what has happened has begun to dawn on me. I feel less confused and realise that no amount of going to morphine-induced sleep will ever change the facts. This is not just a bad dream that I will miraculously wake up from and all will be as it was before. This is my reality.

When I opened my eyes I saw Ro's beaming smile. "Hey," he said. "Your mum has gone to get Martha. She'll be here soon." Martha! This was as equally joyful as it was painful. Joy that she was fine, that I would see her, but pain that I was laying stuck in this hospital bed and could not look after her. This thought flashed over me before leaving again. I was both exhausted and excited to see Martha – her arrival created a momentary distraction from my plight. She was so tiny, cute and dressed so beautifully. I knew that Ruth and Alice had been out buying her gorgeous, tiny, baby clothes.

It was so nice to see Martha but I felt so weak and useless, it wasn't long before I drifted off to sleep with her curled up on my chest. When I woke, Martha was gone.

21st June

This afternoon when I woke, a couple of nurses were checking the charts. One of them smiled at me and said "Hi Wendy, I'm glad you're awake, we've got something exciting to do now." God bless them for trying to make hideous experiences somehow exciting! They left the room and returned with what looked like a bed. "This is a special table," the nurse continued. "We're going to put you on it and then gently tilt it up so that you are upright. This is good for your circulation."

'Okay,' I thought, 'that can't be too bad.' The nurses slid me onto the tilting bed and gradually began to tilt me forwards. Oh my god, it was awful. I felt sick, my head swimming. "Just relax as much as you can," said the nurse, who must have seen the look of horror on my face. I couldn't wait for it to be over. "Not too long, dear," said the other nurse encouragingly. "It's worth it, I promise. You're doing great." After what seemed like an age, but was actually only a few minutes they returned the bed back to horizontal. Gradually my swimming head began to subside and the nausea began to fade. 'I really hope I don't have to do that too often,' I thought, 'and preferably never again!'

22nd June

Mum had the brilliant idea of bringing in the kids' mega-sketcher so that I could write on it and thus communicate. This worked well, although was intensely challenging. I was obsessed with finishing sentences, even when the family had sussed what I wanted. My spelling was phonetic and I would write into the corner and just keep writing and writing. I would go over the top of what I had previously written, so intent on finishing what I had started. This process was both liberating – it opened the channels of communication from no speech, but also frustrating as I simply couldn't remember the words for things. This meant that I needed to describe some things at length in order to communicate something simple.

23rd June

Last night was the longest night I have ever experienced in my entire life. I was filled with fear; feeling like the night was endless. I was awake for long periods in a state of paranoia that I was in the wrong room or that someone was coming to hurt me. There was nothing I could do to escape because I couldn't move. I was absolutely petrified. It felt very dark, and when I did manage to sleep it was fraught with demons. I recall waking in a state of fear, feeling totally isolated and alone. No one was with me and I couldn't even call out for help. The nurses were obviously coming in and out regularly, but it didn't feel like that at all. Every minute felt like hours; it was the worst night of my life!

This morning I felt petrified that I might die. I don't want to die. I felt so fragile. The severity of what had happened hadn't dawned on me until now. I'm really ill. 'I could die at any moment.' I didn't want to tell Ro, as he was being so strong. There came a moment when Mum and I were alone in the room and I just could not contain it any longer. She was doing something on the windowsill and as she turned round and saw my face, she instantly knew something was wrong. "What's wrong, love?" she asked, looking really concerned. I'd been trying to be brave, but her question and concern opened the floodgates. I couldn't stop the tears from pouring down my face. She handed me the mega-sketcher. 'I'm scared I'm going to die,' I wrote.

God bless my mum. She has such a big heart and is always very emotional. She was so strong in that moment. She took my hand, tears streaming down her own face as she looked me in the eye, saying with real determination and belief, "You are not going to die now you've made it this far. I know you are scared darling, but you are going to get better and I'll stay with you until you are, so don't worry." Although she was crying there was such a deep sense of conviction emanating from her that somehow I believed her. She told me afterwards that Ruth was absolutely convinced I would live. Ruth had said to her when she arrived at the hospital for the first time, "Mum, if you have never trusted me before, trust me now. Wendy is going to survive, I just know it!" Ruth has always been known for her psychic tendencies.

As children, Ruth and I were always really close, and would spend hours together playing games outside and inside. I loved spending time with her and always felt safe at school because my big sister was two years above me. Our house was about one mile down a lane from the main housing estate and shops. This meant that whilst we were young we were always reliant on Mum to drive us everywhere. We couldn't just play out in the street with other children. Although we had loads of space, which was brilliant, the flipside was that this sometimes felt isolating. Once we got older and began to have the freedom to cycle or walk to places together, it was great. One day we were walking home and were very close to the house. All of a sudden Ruth grabbed my arm and stopped me in my tracks. "Something is dead," she announced, looking ashen. "Something or someone is dead... I can feel it." She looked totally serious and I was a bit spooked, but started laughing and told her not to be daft. We carried on walking and arrived home. As we walked into the kitchen we were greeted by the sight of our parents, both red-eyed, who told us that our cat had been run over and killed. What freaked me out was that it was killed at exactly the spot where Ruth had stopped me! This rattled me for a bit, but then I eventually forgot about it.

Some years later Ruth was going out with an Australian chap. He had returned to Australia to see his family. She woke me one night in absolute panic and worry saying, "Something is wrong with him. He's ill, he needs an operation." I calmed her down and told her it was just a bad dream and she should go back to sleep. In the morning we had a call to say he had been rushed to hospital and had had an operation. Fortunately, all had gone well and he was fine. I was dumbfounded. How had she done that? How had she known?

Not only had Ruth intuited that there was something seriously wrong with me the day her and Alice had visited Martha and I in the maternity unit, but she also intuited that I would survive. She was absolutely convinced of it. She wrote my mum a beautiful letter that she gave to her on the first day that I was diagnosed, when they had told my family that I was in a life threatening condition, but informing her that I would live. This belief passed from Ruth to my mum, and I know that my mum drew on this invisible strength as she told me that I would make it.

Somehow I absorbed this invisible strength, and as Mum stroked my head, I cried a bit more, but gradually the fear began to subside and I drifted off to sleep. It amazes me how those close to me seem to always know the right things to say, especially Ro, Ruth and Mum. Family, friends and loved ones are so important during times of crisis.

24th June

I felt more mentally awake today than I have so far. Things are becoming a little less fuzzy. I'm beginning to put the pieces together. In order to change the bed sheets the nurses roll me from side to side. It was as one of them said, "Just a bit of cold spray on your bottom, Wendy," that the memory of what I had thought was just a dream returned. The aliens in the space ship must have been my interpretation of the nurses. I suddenly wondered what had happened to my body. I knew that they had to remove my womb, ovaries and some flesh, but I had no idea how much.

As the nurses finished what they were doing and left the room, leaving Ro and I alone, I gestured for the mega-sketcher. I wrote, "What happened to my body?" He took it back from me and started to draw. He drew a torso and then marked out a large area and criss-crossed it. He pointed at the diagram and began to explain. "You see this area here? This is the amount of tissue that they had to remove," he said. I just stared at it in disbelief. It all seemed too much to get my head round.

Martha came to visit again. This coincided with being manoeuvred into a big chair. I wanted to look my best for Martha and insisted that they put on an orange T-shirt I had with me, instead of the hospital gown. It was an incredible palaver to manoeuvre into the T-shirt, let alone the chair! Every tiny movement was totally draining and painful. It was odd because I wasn't actually doing anything but simply being lifted and moved by the nurses. It was an incredible challenge to accomplish and left me feeling even more exhausted, if that was at all possible. I did love seeing Martha though as she makes me feel so happy. For miniscule moments I lose myself in her and forget my predicament. I adore looking at her tiny hands, perfect fingers and beautiful little face, together with feeling her comforting warmth on my chest. I am so grateful that she doesn't have any problems. I don't know how I would cope with that as well as mine.

25th–29th June

The days have passed, mostly with me sleeping for long periods. There continues to be regular trips to surgery for dressing changes and this is due to the extent of the wounds and in case any further surgery is required to remove any diseased flesh.

Although I have stabilised, there are serious concerns over the deterioration of my bowel. The bowel condition worsened so another operation was performed to create a fistula. This is where a piece of the bowel lower down is brought to the outside of the body. It's so undignified because it is faeces that leak from this part of the bowel. It stinks and it's so large that they do not have an appropriate bag to contain it. It leaks everywhere and I hate it!

Ruth's instincts kicked in again and she was convinced that the surgeons needed to do something more otherwise I would die. She was disappointed at herself for not saying anything or forewarning anyone right at the start when first sensing I was ill. Her 'knowing' from that time gave her strength and courage to speak up. When my family met with the surgeons to discuss my progress Ruth told them that they had to operate. The surgeons were reluctant to because I was already so weak, but Ruth said that my bowel was poisoning me. She begged them to operate to give me the chance I needed.

The surgeons operated to create an ileostomy. This acts to bypass the bowel in order to let it rest and recover. They made an incision, quite high up – about three fingers above my belly button – which leaks into a bag. The bag gets filled with green bile and is changed fairly frequently. Just how undignified can one's life become? It's very odd to be in a state of total dependency on others just to stay alive. I hate the bag. I hate the fact that my bodily fluids are on the outside and not on the inside where they should be.

The surgeons have also begun to take skin from my thighs to graft onto my torso. These are the beginnings of 'sealing me back up.' This procedure is both painful and irritating, not just the area that is grafted but also the donor site. The donor site is initially intensely sore for a few days, stinging like a severe graze, and then it becomes constantly itchy for a few days. Thankfully, it is over within a two-week period but, unfortunately, it is a process that needs to be repeated in order to cover such a large area.

30th June

Katy and Amy are coming to visit and I can't wait to see them. The doctors have adjusted the tracheostomy so that I can now speak. I have to place my finger over the tube so when I attempt to speak, words will come out. It freaks me out, it's very weird. It takes a ton of effort and I sound like Stephen Hawking!

It was so amazing to see Katy and Amy. It's been ages. Katy came straight up to me and took my hand. Bless her; it was so lovely to see her. I had to fight to hold back the tears; it must have been so traumatic for them, wondering what was happening to their Mummy. Amy, on the other hand, held back. She looked really scared, quite crest-fallen, and was afraid to come too close. I understand it must be very difficult for them.

Ro was amazing as usual, being all chipper and playful with them and attempting to lighten the whole situation. Being kids they were quickly bored and restless, so Ro said he'd take them to the café for cake. As they headed to the door I summoned the courage to attempt to speak, placed my finger over the tube and said, "I love you Katy and Amy." The robotic sound was odd but they were so excited that I could speak. Amy sent a shy little smile in my direction before they bounded out the door.

4th July

The physiotherapist came to make some plaster cast ankle splints. He's called Simon and has also given me some exercises to do. The splints are designed to hold my feet in a flexed position in order to minimise difficulty with walking once I get back on my feet. I have to wear them for a couple of hours several times a day. It's really quite uncomfortable and I don't like them. When Simon came back in the afternoon to put them on again and make me do some more exercises I pretended to be asleep – I just couldn't face it. The pain and discomfort of having pressure on my feet is horrible. I did have another session with them later on and although I understand they are doing what's best for me, to help my recovery and not create further problems down the line – it sucks!!

6th July

Kevin from Abbey ward (that's the plastic surgery ward) arrived to manage my feet. He deals with the VAC dressings, which were used on my torso wound, right after the first surgery. Basically, it's a sponge that fills the wound, then a tube that is connected to a pump. The sponge is wrapped with plastic to create an airtight seal. It helps to speed the wound healing up and also to reduce the size of it.

Ro told me that he'd seen quite a lot of Kevin, as he was heavily involved in my care right from the start. He came to apply VAC dressings on the insteps of both feet. He also gave my feet a really good clean, in between all my toes, which was a bit painful but okay. I hope this helps, as it seems to be procedure after procedure at the moment. I keep trusting that it's all for the best but with no idea of how I will end up. Kevin was very chatty and friendly and he is about the same age as Ro and I. I enjoyed listening to the humour when Kevin and Ro chatted.

My dad came to visit. I don't see my dad very often as he lives in France and we have had a fairly estranged relationship for many years. He's not good with illness, never has been and he always struggles with emotions, especially in expressing them. I always knew he loved me because I could see it in his eyes, but he would never say it. One day when I was eighteen and we were in the pub (one of his favourite places), I looked him the eye and said, "Tell me you love me." I didn't break eye contact. After stuttering for a moment he mumbled, "I love you."

When he arrived he walked over to me, took my hand, leaned in close, kissed me on the forehead and then whispered, "The only one (as in daughter) who has ever made me tell her I love her, and the only one who has frightened me to death." That one sentence spoke a thousand words.

7th July

"Would you like to take a trip outside into the garden?" asked one of the lovely nurses. "It's a beautiful day; how would you like a bit of summer?" The thought of the sunshine sounded wonderful, although I was confused as to how I would do such a thing. She explained that they would get some portable oxygen and move all the equipment so that I could be wheeled outside while still on my bed.

The preparation for our expedition to the garden took ages, but eventually I was being wheeled out from the only four walls I had seen for the last few weeks. It felt strange to be in public, the mill of people in the corridors and the activity of other people's day-to-day lives. I had been so preoccupied with my own little bubble and myself; I had forgotten the existence of the world outside.

Ro was with me, walking alongside the bed, chatting happily with the nurse as we made our way along the corridor and into the lift. Ro started telling me all about the different little gardens and how they had unique themes.

Emerging from the lift we travelled further along a corridor before exiting double doors into the garden. The sunlight hit my face, which was blindingly bright. I had to close my eyes because they hurt. The warmth on my face felt nice for a moment, but then I suddenly felt completely overwhelmed and just wanted to return to the safety of my room. "Thank you, but can we please go back?" I asked. I was feeling slightly guilty at the level of preparation and effort that had resulted in me spending about one minute in the garden! The nurse, however, was gorgeous. She was smiling at me and said, "Bit much? Of course we can."

8th July

I lay in the bed pondering what my body looked like now, following the destruction by the disease. The dressings could now be changed while I was awake, and so were being carried out on the ward. Although the thought of seeing what I was left with following the surgery frightened me, I knew it was time to stop closing my eyes when the dressings were being changed. Instead I decided to be brave and take a look. Fortunately for me, the nurses changed the dressings in stages, which presented me with the opportunity to peek at one part of it rather than the whole thing. As the nurse was changing the dressing on the top right-hand side, I peeked at my mutilated body and saw red, angry, puffy and odd-looking skin staring back at me. I closed my eyes as I couldn't believe this was my body. I hated it. It looked so completely grotesque, that in that moment, I could not imagine how I would ever feel comfortable with my body again. Despair overtook me – my throat tightened and the tears welled in my eyes before coursing down my cheeks. It looks disgusting. I look hideous and I hate it!

Not only do I have this massive area of destruction to my torso, but my legs are also severely scarred and damaged. Red, raw thighs from their donation of skin for the grafts to my torso; several holes in my inner calves, blackened toe tips and huge indents on both insteps as a result of septicaemia. The doctors have told me not to worry about the toe tips, as they will just drop off. Oh! That's alright then, I won't worry about that!! I have always been super-squeamish, so dealing with all this disfigurement is a real challenge. I spent a few tear-filled hours flitting between utter despair at the awfulness of it all, total gratitude to still be alive and complete and total exhaustion where there is nothing left to even care.

A few hours later the plastic surgeon came in. "Hey," he said. "What are the red eyes about?" "I look horrible," I replied, as the tears pricked in my eyes and flowed once more. What he said next really surprised me. "Yep," he agreed. "It's the worst thing you will ever see, but it will improve. When you get stronger we can do some reconstructive surgery. We can expand your normal skin, then remove the grafts and join this normal skin together. This means you will end up with a smiley scar on your tummy." This made me feel better. The thought that there was much they could do to make it look better gave me hope. I imagined a neat and tidy smiley scar on my tummy. I can deal with that.

10th July

I could feel the warmth of Ro's hand holding mine as I began to wake up. It was hard to wake up, I felt so tired. As my eyes swam into focus I could instantly see the worried look on Ro's face. He must have realised that I was on to him because he squeezed my hand and said, "Hello, Love. Your chest might be hurting. You've got a chest infection but you're going to be fine." I didn't feel any worse; I think it would have been hard to feel any worse at this point. I did feel really tired though. It was a struggle to keep my eyes open. In fact, I'll just close them and rest. Sleep took me again.

I could hear quiet voices as I woke up. I opened my eyes and there was Ro. He still looked really worried but he beamed a smile at me. "Hey, Beautiful," he greeted me. "Nice sleep?" I nodded, still feeling quite sleepy. "Simon's here," he said, nodding towards the physiotherapist. 'Oh no,' I thought. 'What's Simon going to do?' Everything that was linked to Simon was either hard work, painful or both.

"Hello," said Simon. "How are you feeling?"

"Okay," I muttered. "Still feeling sleepy."

Simon smiled. He began to move towards the bed, wheeling this contraption. "I've got this for you," he said. "It's going to help your chest. I'll show you how it works."

Simon manoeuvred the contraption nearer to the bed. 'The Bird' he called it. He plugged it in before starting to explain what it was. "You put this mask part over your mouth and breathe five deep breaths, as deep as you can," he explained. "This is really going to help your chest and make you feel better. Let's get you a little more upright," he said.

Ro already had the electric control in his hand and pressed the button to bring me to a more upright position. "It's a bit noisy," he said, as he turned the machine on and it burst into life, making a very loud noise. It sounded like a petrol lawn mower. Simon handed me the mask and then helped me place it over my mouth and nose. "Okay," he instructed. "Now take five, slow, deep breaths."

I started to take the first breath, phew! It was so hard to breathe, it made me realise just how shallow my breathing had become. A pain shot through my chest, I winced, but continued to do as I was told. Five breaths later, Simon smiled and removed the mask. "Well done," he said, beaming. "That was great. Now just rest there a minute. You should feel the urge to cough pretty soon."

"COUGH!" A surge of fear swept through me. 'Can I do that? What about my stomach? What about my intestines resting outside of my body? Will I damage something? Burst something? Simon must have seen the look of panic on my face. "It's perfectly fine," he reassured. "It's absolutely what your body needs right now."

There are times in life when you realise that your body is actually in control and not you. It takes over and does the perfect thing that it needs to do. This was one of those times. Who would have thought that something that is so taken for granted, something so simple as a cough could be such a challenge? I felt the urge to cough but didn't feel like I could. Suddenly, I felt my chest tighten and something begin to rise up. All of a sudden my chest contracted and a small cough happened. I was so scared that I would burst something vital and die in an instant, but I was still alive and my chest was tightening again. I coughed again, this time with a little more force than the first cough. Simon smiled, "Well done," he said. He reached over and flicked the switch to turn the machine on again. As it hummed into action he passed me the mask. "Another five breaths, please," he instructed with a smile.

Five breaths later and I felt exhausted. As Simon took the mask my arm collapsed on the bed. Then my chest tightened and I coughed again. The next cough brought with it a surprise, a disgusting mouthful of phlegm! Simon was very excited. (Hospital people make me laugh at their excitement towards body fluids, parts and goings on. Brilliant isn't it? That which 'Joe Public' finds disgusting they find fascinating, and I guess for them, it often signifies positive things that reflect the body's return to health). "Fantastic," he said, grabbing the suction pipe to suck the phlegm from my mouth.

More coughing followed along with more phlegm. Simon had me do 'The Bird' a third time, and then after that bout of coughing and phlegm-ing, he told me I could rest. He left Ro and I the instructions on how to use 'The Bird' four times a day. He stressed the importance of it. "I know it's hard work for you," he empathised, "but it's really important for your chest. Trust me, it will really help to get your chest clear and make you feel better." He left, saying he'd be back later to check all was well.

I was exhausted and soon drifted off to sleep.

13th July

My chest is feeling a lot better today. I've slept a lot over the last few days. I am very grateful to The Bird. As much as it is unpleasant, exhausting and that I dislike it, it has definitely helped.

14th July

Ro came in with a big grin on his face. "Look what I've got her," he said. Katy's seventh birthday had just passed and she was coming to visit. He'd gone out to get her a present. He produced this big box and I could see it was a remote-controlled car. "She'll love that," I said, as a smile and a tear simultaneously met the thought of Katy and Amy. I really miss them and have seen them very infrequently. I've been told they are doing fine, but I worry about how they're really coping. They must be wondering what on earth is going on with their mum. And poor Amy looked so scared at the last visit… that was really difficult.

Katy and Amy arrived in the afternoon. It was so lovely to see them and Amy was less timid, thank goodness. I guess it helps that I can speak a little, am less swollen and there are less scary tubes and wires. Perhaps I look a little more like me. The birthday present was a great choice by Ro. Katy was delighted with it and I felt so happy watching her drive it round my room. The nurses were really lovely with them. I am always overjoyed to see the girls, but it is difficult because they are so lively and I become exhausted so quickly. Ro's great though as when he saw I looked exhausted he said, "Hey, come on girls, let's drive that car down to the café and get a drink and some cake," and shot me a mischievous smile. It's a bit naughty to drive the remote-controlled car in the corridor but Katy and Amy quite clearly loved the idea. It had their total focus and, giggling, they left the room. I heard the whirr of the remote-controlled car as they travelled down the corridor and I closed my eyes with a smile on my face.

16th July

The major achievement today is that the tracheostomy has been removed and I am now just on an oxygen mask. It is such a relief to have the tracheostomy out as it was beginning to be very uncomfortable. I was equally scared and excited that they were removing it, but it came out quite easily and was not too bad adjusting to the mask. I was really quite worried at first that I wouldn't be able to breathe properly or get enough oxygen. All was going well until this afternoon; while the nurses were changing the bedding; the mask fell off as they rolled me. I freaked out and immediately thought I was going to die without it. The nurse was really calming, talking me down off the ledge, whilst gently replacing the mask. I can do it. I can breathe all by myself and even survive without the oxygen mask. Serious progress! It also means I can speak properly again – very liberating.

The best thing has been another visit from Martha. Wow, she is so utterly gorgeous; a dinky little bundle, so peaceful and calm. I am so grateful that Mum is visiting her lots. Ro's mum's also been visiting her regularly. It's wonderful to know that she is receiving love from the family at this time when I cannot be there for her. With the aid of pillows and some helping hands, I am able to give her a cuddle on my chest. I even attempted to bottle feed her. It's quite a challenge but it does act as an amazing distraction.

Ruth and Alice have also visited her and she continues to be a fabulously dressed baby, thanks to everyone. Apparently, the nurses in the special care baby unit have been wonderful too. They have made a Martha Diary for me so that I will get to see the bits that I have missed.

17th July

Today's challenge is to eat. I really don't feel remotely hungry or in the least bit interested in food. I seem to feel in a constant state of nausea. Although I don't feel like eating, the doctors encouraged me to try, so I did my best. The offering of the day was minced chicken... who on earth minces chicken? I don't think anything would have tasted particularly good given the circumstances, but this tasted foul (excuse the pun!) I only ate a few tiny mouthfuls. It really is the most incredible experience being this incapable. There are so many things I take for granted. Simple and ordinary daily things we all do without a second thought, they are all suddenly such massive challenges. The act of eating is yet another one. It is virtually impossible. It wasn't long before I vomited and the attempt to eat solid food was abandoned.

It's also Ro's birthday. Mum purchased a card and gift for him from me. What a way to spend your birthday!

18th July

Ruth visited which gave me the chance to find out something I'd been pondering, but was almost too embarrassed to ask. I knew I'd lost my womb and ovaries and I knew from Ro's sketch that the tissue loss was extensive and low down – but just how much flesh and tissue had they removed? I'll get to the point... what about my clitoris? Had it been removed as well? The perfect moment miraculously appeared today when the room was empty apart from Ruth and I. Her reply was so typically Ruth that it instantly brought humour to my oh-so deep turmoil. It lightened the load in a moment.

"Don't worry about that," she said. "I already checked and yes, you have still got it. I asked them after they did the first surgery. When they said it was still intact I said, "Well, thank god for that, otherwise she may as well be dead!"

I love my sister for her blunt humour and at least there was one thing that I hadn't lost.

19th July

The reappearance of some normality

It's so strange being bedridden and unable to get up and move around. I don't like being washed because it means I have to face the monstrosity of my body, but I do love having my hair washed. It's a real treat. The nurses gave Ro this flattish plastic tray that means he can wash my hair while I am lying down. It feels so lovely, the warm water pouring over my head. Not only is it a luxury to have clean hair, but also the sensation of the water is so wonderfully soothing and relaxing.

This afternoon while Mum and I were chatting, I stretched my arm up and was faced with a forest of underarm hair. "Crikey, Mum!" I gasped. "Could you shave my armpits?" What a funny request from a 29-year-old woman to her mother. My mum's face was an absolute picture; she was overjoyed. I know this was because it was a sign that I was feeling better. The fact that I was even bothered to have hair under my arms.

Chapter 4
Abbey Ward

20th July

"They are moving you onto Abbey ward," announced Ro. "That's Kevin's ward. It's the plastic surgery one." I could tell that he was delighted; moving out of high dependency was a great step. I had been in intensive care for six weeks. The thought of moving onto a 'normal' ward felt really good to me as well. It felt like a big step in being closer to going home.

I'm making good progress. My sides are mostly all grafted now and it has all taken well. I still have the bags though and the tube in my nose, but I'm getting stronger. I'm also feeling slightly more alive with each passing day, although I know I still have a long way to go. The ITU nurses were also very excited; they care so much, it's very special.

21st July

I'm now on Abbey ward. I was a little worried as it felt a bit like coming out of a bubble. Now I'm here it feels really good. I'm in a private side room, which is brilliant. The idea of being on a ward was very unappealing and quite daunting. However, my door looks out over the main reception and I can see people coming and going which is very enjoyable to watch. It's nice to see life again, the hustle and bustle of a ward.

There is a pregnant lady who has walked past my door several times today. She walks past really slowly; I wonder what her story is.

It all seems to be happening today. I have moved out of intensive care and the other major news is that Martha is ready to come home. Mum informed me of this when she visited.

A rush of excitement coursed through me initially because, of course, it means Martha is doing really well. This was swiftly followed by a wave of sadness. My little baby is ready to go home and yet I won't be there to look after her. When Mum told me I forced a smile, but I knew she could read me like a book because you can't fake a smile with your eyes. As I looked into hers I could see the tinge of sadness there as well. I guess she was thinking similar thoughts to me.

"I'm going to look after her so that Ro can be with you," she said. "I'll bring her in every day to see you."

I have no doubts that Martha and I will bond. I think if she was my first child I might be worried about this, but I feel confident as a mother thanks to Katy and Amy. The most important thing is that Martha is strong enough to go home and that, luckily, Mum is able to take time off work to be with her. She will be able to care for her and give her that loving, daily 'Mother bond' that I cannot give myself right now. The hardest part is missing out on looking after my tiny baby. I had been so looking forward to breastfeeding her. I'd loved the special closeness of this experience that I'd shared with Katy and Amy. I was missing out on so many cuddles, on caring for my new baby, all the firsts! Suddenly, I thought about the beautiful new pram we had chosen. I wouldn't be the first to push Martha in it. An even worse thought, 'Would I ever push her in it?' My brave face and rational approach went out the window, as I couldn't hold back the tears that ran down my cheeks.

Mum's eyes watered and she gave me a hug. "I love you," she said. I sometimes forget that this is tough for all of us, not just me. "Thank you, Mum," I said. "I really am grateful and it does mean that I will now get to see her every day."

22nd July

6 am – I'm so sad this morning, I can't stop crying. It all seems way too much. The only thought that I have in my head is, 'Why me?' I can't bear it. I just need Ro. I hope he comes soon.

7.30 am – One of the very kind nurses just came in and tried to talk to me. She could obviously see I'm upset. She was lovely but I don't want to talk to anyone else, just Ro. I have asked her to call him and ask him to come as soon as he can.

Finally, Ro arrived. I don't know how he does it but somehow, he makes me feel so much better. He seems to be able to say just the right things. He brought in a magazine with a story about a woman who had also had necrotising fasciitis and had made an amazing recovery. He came across it while I was sedated and read it to me. I've not seen him cry once, but there was a point when he was reading that he choked up. He stopped, squeezed my hand, took a moment and then continued reading.

When he'd finished I looked at him and said, "You always say the right things. How do you know what to say?"

"I don't know," he replied. "I don't think about it, I just say things."

"Well, they are perfect," I smiled weakly. "I don't know what I'd do without you."

23rd July - No one understands!

Crikey, I've gone from extreme sadness to extreme anger. I'm so angry today! It is making me so mad that everyone tries to be so understanding. They come in and say nice things but they have no idea of what I am experiencing – no idea of what I'm trying to deal with, let alone what I am attempting to come to terms with. How can they? Not that I want them to really understand. I wouldn't wish this on anyone.

It's the same question as yesterday. I'm angry that this has happened to me. Why me? What did I do? I was just really happy, feeling I'd found my soul mate, with two beautiful daughters and about to be having a baby together to add to our family. This should be a happy time, a time of celebration. Instead I am lying here flat on my back, attempting to overcome a life threatening, severely disfiguring illness. No one deserves this.

Abbey ward have been amazing and very empathetic. I guess this is all part of the struggle and journey of recovery; all part of coming to terms with what has happened to me. They asked if I would like to see someone who has been through something similar. I said that yes, I would. A lady called Kate is coming to visit me. She didn't have necrotising fasciitis but had septicaemia instead and lost a number of her fingers. I hope it helps because right now I feel terrible.

25th July

Seeing Kate was incredible, really helpful and healing. She is such a lovely woman that in some weird way it's put my problems into perspective. I had not fully understood the consequences and devastating effects of septicaemia until now. It did not occur to me when I lost my toe tips, some tendons and the flesh of my insteps that I could have come out a lot worse and lost not only more of my toes and skin of my feet, but also my fingers, hands and – what seems even worse than that – my nose! I am so grateful to have come away with just the loss of seven toe tips, scarring and the idea of being somewhat flat-footed. While I was sedated my arms were in slings and became blotchy, but my mum used to massage them every day. I wonder if this helped to prevent some of the destruction.

I also realised in seeing Kate that I will easily be able to cover up all my scarring and disfigurement, whereas she cannot cover her hands. She was so vibrant and really lifted my spirits. I am so grateful to her for that. The fact that she had got on with her life and was generally happy is really inspiring. She has also given me renewed hope at a point when I was nearly out of it. The anger seems to have subsided. Somehow, seeing Kate has softened something, or perhaps it is the renewed hope that will enable me to carry on and be able to live a successful, normal life.

26th–31st July - Life on Abbey

The days on Abbey ward are whiled away with some sort of normality. Mum comes in every day with Martha. She always brings her in when a feed is due so that I can feed her. I love the Martha moments; they somehow make each day more bearable. It really is something to look forward to. I love all the little clothes that Mum, Ruth and Alice have bought for her. She always looks so adorable.

Since I am still bedbound and am only able to lie on my back, it is still awkward to feed her; I have difficulty positioning her in a way that is comfortable for both of us. I have an electric bed and can be elevated so that I am more upright, but I keep slipping down the bed. When this happens the nurses come and pull me back up on the sheets. Funny old process really. It is so odd to be so heavily dependent on others for all that I need. When I was in ITU there were moments of realising this, but it seems so much more apparent now. I guess I was so ill that I didn't think about it too much before. This makes me think that it must be a good sign to be even thinking about being independent, even if it's the thought that I am not!

The ileostomy bag bothers me. As it is right where I would have naturally positioned Martha, instead she is always quite high up on my chest. However, where there's a will there's a way and so we have worked out positions with the aid of multiple pillows. It's hard to wind her, partly because of the position but also the fact that I am so weak; even to hold the bottle while she is on a pillow has been exhausting. I think it is helping for me to regain some of my strength though. I feel so much better. I am now able to stay awake for much longer periods during the day. We have a TV in the room so that helps to pass some of the time. Ro and I have got into watching the re-runs of Quincy M.E. (a late 70s–early 80s medical drama) in the afternoons. It's a great distraction and a chance to lose myself for a while.

The physiotherapist now visits on a more regular basis and has given me a variety of exercises to do. He has rigged up this triangle thing that hangs down from above me at about chest height, so that I can pull myself back up the bed when I slip down. This has been so liberating as it's great not having to wait for a couple of nurses to be free to be able to come and hoist me back up the bed every time. The most recent addition to my exercises are these long elastic bands, a bit like you get in exercise classes, which are tied to the head of my bed. Several times a day I have to stretch the band out as far as I can. I find it very hard as it takes massive effort and I cannot quite straighten my arm out yet.

1st August

I made a friend. The pregnant lady that I have seen going past my door several times a day came in and said, "Hello." Having seen Martha with my mum she couldn't help but say, "hi." She's a lovely lady and has to deal with cancer in her groin whilst being pregnant. She told me that she had refused a particular drug because she was trying to minimise them as much as possible. She obviously needs to care for her unborn baby whilst also caring for herself. The deal the doctors made was for her to do a certain amount of walking each day, hence the regular trips past my door.

It was nice to make a friend; there is so much going on for other people. It has reminded me that other people have problems and challenges as well. I am not the only one. Odd that I could forget that whilst being in a hospital! It felt good to be reminded, and also to lose my own trauma for a moment and empathise with someone else.

2nd August

The excitement of today was Katy and Amy coming to visit with Alice. She is looking after them for three weeks during the summer holidays. It's so kind of her and she even got some bunk beds for her spare room to make it special for them. I couldn't wait to see them. Amy was brilliant, she trotted in and the first thing she saw was the band on the head of the bed. "What's this?" she questioned as she grabbed it and effortlessly stretched it right out to the end of my bed. I couldn't believe it! I had thought the bands were really tough. Seeing little five-year-old Amy stretch it to the end of the bed with absolute ease, it dawned on me just how incredibly weak I still am.

Katy and Amy are doing well, bless them. I cannot imagine what it must be like for them. Amy has been a little destructive with a couple of things, however. Alice told me that she cut up one of her school dresses. It must be very confusing for a five-year-old to deal with. They have a new baby sister and their dad has a new girlfriend (who also has a daughter). This must be challenging enough when you're seven and five, let alone having your mum seriously ill in hospital as well. It makes me sad. I wish I could be there for them.

It was a successful visit though, and so wonderful to see them. Mum came with Martha, so for a moment I had all my family together. I wonder when I will be able to go home and we will be together again? I have no idea when this will be. Part of me longs for it but I am also really scared, not imagining how on earth I would cope. I loved seeing Amy and Katy holding Martha. They seem really delighted with her, so that's comforting.

Unfortunately, I've been feeling quite sick for quite a few days now. I hate nausea and there is nothing I can do about it. Hopefully it will pass soon. I've got this horrible, thick tube coming out of my nose. It's got bile in it and I can see the green out of the corner of my eye... not a pretty sight.

3rd August

The fistula is really distressing. Well, not really the thing itself, it doesn't hurt or anything, but it's the leakage. I feel so disgusting! There is no standard bag that is big enough to contain it so on a regular basis it leaks everywhere. As I stated before, it is really disgusting and it stinks. I haven't eaten anything for weeks so I don't understand why it smells so bad. I always believed the smell of faeces came from food. I have been having liquid food intravenously administered because I can't keep anything down myself. Today when it leaked I burst into tears. Ro gave me a hug and then with a, "Right, back in a minute," he disappeared out of the room. He returned shortly with Kevin who had a selection of bags, some tape and a pair of scissors. Kevin put all the things down on the table and said, "There you go Ro, that's what we've got. Have a go."

"I'm going to make a bag that works," Ro announced, and immediately started sifting through the possible selection. It wasn't long before he'd made a bag and disappeared again to find Kevin. Kevin returned, smiled and exclaimed, "Nice one," before fixing the newly created bag into place. Hey presto, it didn't leak! It was so amazing. I always loved Ro's practical approach to finding solutions rather than dwelling on problems. What would I do without him?

Ro also gave my hair a wash. I love this so much; the warm water cascading over my head always feels so amazing. I can't imagine what it is like for him, day after day attending to my very demanding needs. Not so much physically, although the bag was genius, but definitely emotionally. He is always so strong and somehow able to say the perfect thing. He told me that he was just glad I was alive. That he had promised to look after me, even if I was severely disabled. In the first few days of intensive care he had my wedding ring on his finger and all the time it was there he felt I was okay. One afternoon he went outside to get fresh air and was sitting on a bench when my ring fell off. Initially he couldn't find it and was searching frantically. He was becoming more fearful with each second that passed. Finally he found it, breathed a huge sigh of relief and replaced it on his finger. He is not religious, but also told me that in those early days, as he walked past the chapel each day, he would look in and say that he was grateful I was alive. He told me that these little rituals and beliefs somehow helped. How, when all else seems bleak we seek solace in something greater than ourselves.

I feel so special that he loves me so much. Somehow he helps to make all of this more bearable.

I still feel sick and have had this underlying nausea for most of the day.

5th August

Yesterday I went to surgery for more skin grafting. Coming round from the anaesthetic is such a horrible process for me. Not just that it makes me feel totally wiped out, but also I get so cold that it takes ages to warm up. I end up completely wrapped in about ten blankets, with one rolled into a sausage and placed around the top of my head. This cold lasts for what feels like a lifetime before, suddenly, my body feels like it has burst into flames and I become completely boiling hot. Gradually, that subsides and eventually my temperature returns to normal.

The surgeons are pleased with my progress, which is great and encouraging.

The other big news is that the catheter has been removed. The mixed feelings around all of these milestones are so interesting. Part of me meets it with fear and trepidation and another part of me is overjoyed that that particular part is over. To wee for myself is really quite a major milestone!

My usual psychological squeamish part was having a field day with the thought of the catheter being removed. I tried not to think about it too much, but as I have found with most of these things, the actual removal was over quickly and wasn't too uncomfortable. I am grateful to the nurses that they do many things with as little pre-warning as they can. They came and told me it was ready to come out and then promptly got on with it.

I now have the indignity of having to use a bedpan. The return of the sensations to urinate was quite tricky at first; I kept thinking I needed to go only to find that the urge had disappeared. It's quite a palaver to be able to get onto the bedpan in the right position and upright enough. It takes a ton of effort and exhausts me but, hey, it's all progress and a step closer to home, although I have no idea when that will be.

6th August

Well, after a day of not knowing if I needed to wee or not and misreading my body in that mostly I didn't, I spent the whole night needing to wee every hour. It's left me feeling really tired because I'd just manage to get to sleep before I'd wake again and need a wee. Then there would be the bell, the time for the nurse to come and manoeuvre me onto the pan, the time to wee, the time to get off the bedpan and settle back to sleep, only to feel like I was immediately awake and needing to go again! Excuse the details – but properly going as well – not just a trickle. I hope it settles down soon.

7th August

Another night of the same pattern with urinating. I don't seem to go at all during the day but then virtually all through the night, I need to go six or seven times. It's so weird. It's like my body has turned this daytime process into a night-time one. On the one hand it's great that it is all functioning properly by itself but on the other hand it's so tiring having to wake up for it in the night. It also pisses me off (excuse the pun) because it's difficult to get to sleep in the first place. I wonder how long this pattern will go on?

8th August

The mornings consist of early breakfast, the nurses administering tablets and doctors' rounds. I like observing the comings and goings of breakfast and the drugs round. It's a relief to see a new day arrive, as I don't sleep particularly well and wake many times throughout the night. This always makes the nights seem long. This being made even worse by the addition of the recent nocturnal need to wee every hour, which happened again last night. I don't eat breakfast as I am still on the liquid food and, as I have been feeling sick every day, I have not been taking the tablets for pain relief. They just make me feel even more nauseous and I can't keep them down. I feel okay without them so it doesn't seem to matter.

I now cannot recall the last time I *didn't* feel sick. The thick tube in my nose drives me nuts. I can still see the hideous green bile in it out of the corner of my eye. I don't think that helps me with feeling nauseous, it probably just adds to it. As I mentioned before, I've always been quite psychologically squeamish; the thought of pain making my stomach do somersaults and the addition of this green goo permanently in my peripheral vision doesn't help either. I tell you, I cannot wait until they take the thing out.

The nurses pop in each morning to check on me and have a chat. They really are lovely and I feel that I have quite a bond with a number of the regular ones. It's nice to get to know them. This morning I noticed there was a different atmosphere on the ward. As one of the nurses came in to say good morning to me I noticed she was wearing lipstick. She beamed a smile at me and asked excitedly, "Have you seen George Clooney?" I chuckled, "What? What's going on?"

"It's change-over day," she replied with a huge grin. "The doctors rotate round and there is a new one who looks like George Clooney."

"Wow!" I laughed. "I look forward to seeing him."

That morning, many of the nurses were more chipper than normal, nothing like a bit of eye candy to brighten your day. Not long afterwards I spied him at the front desk. He did look very much like George Clooney... nice! I enjoyed the view for a moment before he disappeared off to his duties.

9th August

Last night my level of dependency on others reached a whole new level. I still have the usual needing to wee hourly throughout the night and, after I woke on one occasion, I reached for the button to ring the nurse. As I was sleepy it unfortunately knocked off the bed. I didn't know what to do. I couldn't get it, couldn't reach the main bell, couldn't move and needed a wee. What was I going to do in a room with the door shut? I called out, "Hello," but couldn't hear anybody. I called out again, "Hello, can someone help me? I've dropped my bell." I listened intently but still couldn't hear anybody. I really needed a wee now, the situation was becoming more urgent and I really didn't want to wet the bed.

I called out again, met no response and then a tear trickled down my face. This was nuts; all I need to do is wee and yet here I am helplessly lying in a bed unable to get up and go to the toilet. I was just about to resign myself to having no other option but to wet the bed when I heard a noise. "Hello, Hello, I need help," I continued to call out desperately. The door handle started to move and a nurse popped her head around the door. "You okay in here?" Oh my, the relief!

"I'm desperate for a wee," I said with urgency. "No problem," was the response, and it wasn't too long before the second relief came thanks to that lovely nurse. She gave me my bell back and secured it in a way that, if knocked off, would still be reachable. The situation turned from one of disaster and despair into one of humour. What an odd time I was having in my life! An adult reverted to total dependency on others for all of my basic needs, much like a young baby.

12th August

The plastic surgeon came and spoke to Ro and I about me going home for a spell to get stronger. I needed to do this before returning to have the operation that would correct my bowel and seal the hole in my tummy. The thought of this filled me with dread; I hate those bags, but even more importantly I cannot tolerate feeling sick any longer. This incessant nausea has gone on for nearly a whole month now and I virtually begged him to do the operation as soon as possible. After conferring with the bowel surgeon, they have agreed, and an operation has been scheduled for next week. This means I will also finally be waving goodbye to the hideous green tube of bile!

They have told me that in order to repair the bowel, they will need to use something to seal in the lower bowel and repair the remaining hole in my lower abdomen. For this they will use a piece of pigskin to seal the lower bowel and then take a piece of my left thigh to seal the wound. As far as I am concerned the operation is going to be a success. There is no way that I am going home with a colostomy bag.

18th August

I am pleased to report the surgeons carried out a successful operation yesterday. Most of the bowel had recovered and repaired, which is amazing news. They only needed to remove a small section, which will not adversely affect me.

When I came round in the recovery unit Mum was there, stroking my head. She looked really worried. It was *really* hard to wake up, I just kept going back to sleep. Each time I came round Mum was still there. Unfortunately there had been an outbreak of MRSA on Abbey ward, and given how weak I was, the recovery team didn't want me returning to the ward. There was talk of me going to the intensive care ward. This felt like a relief because I really did feel incredibly weak. In the end I stayed in recovery all night with my beautiful mum by my side at every moment.

I returned to Abbey ward this afternoon. I am praying to god that the sickness is over and my bowel is recovered enough to function normally again. I feel a lot stronger today compared to yesterday, but still incredibly weak. Mum confessed to me that she had been really worried following the operation and through the night because it had taken me so long to come round, plus my temperature had been incredibly high.

The first task is to fart! Being British and a lady we spend most of our lives discreetly breaking wind because it's not something a lady does. Mind you, those that know me well would surely have some comments about me being a lady and discreetly farting. Plus, farting was a huge source of amusement in our house as a child because my dad thought it was hysterical. Suddenly the tables are turned and the doctors, consultants and ever-so-caring nurses are popping in and asking me with very serious faces, "Have you farted yet?" For me, this raises a mix of embarrassment and humour, coupled with a strong desire to fart because this means things are beginning to work and the operation was successful. It also means that I can begin to eat again, although I will definitely not be having minced chicken!

19th August

No farts yet but thankfully the nausea has gone. I cannot tell you what a huge relief that is!

20th August

Big news! The much-awaited fart has happened. It was such an exciting occasion and everyone was delighted. For the first time in ten weeks some real food has passed my lips. It was so hard to eat. Even the smallest of mouthfuls took ages to chew and swallow. I have no appetite and yet it is needed for me to consume huge amounts of calories for my healing. They have given me some special calorie-rich milkshakes but they also taste rich and it's a serious struggle to drink them. A couple of sips and I feel full! I tried a few occasions to take more past this full feeling, but that doesn't work because I just instantly vomit.

I hadn't really thought that much about going home; it was only when the doctors had said they wanted to send me home to get stronger before doing the bowel operation that I had even begun to consider it as a serious possibility. Prior to that it seemed like this distant idea.

21st August

How odd that Katy is sleeping below me tonight. Mum appeared this afternoon looking worried; I instantly knew something was wrong as I saw her approaching.

"Everything is fine," was her opening line, "but Katy has had a seizure and is downstairs on the children's ward being checked out. She's okay though and is now resting."

She told me that, in the morning, Katy had been coming back from her Granny and Granddad's in Cornwall, where her and Amy had been visiting, to their dad's in Exeter when it had started. Amy had piped up from the back seat, "Why is Katy blowing bubbles?" Katy's grandparents had taken her straight to the hospital in Exeter. The seizure didn't last too long and she was now resting in the children's ward.

Katy had been diagnosed with benign rolandic epilepsy a few years back. This type comes usually at night and fortunately the seizures are very infrequent. I was just relieved that she was okay and the odd highlight was that I got to see her in the afternoon after she had rested and recovered a little. The hospital decided to keep her in overnight to monitor her and just make sure she was okay. Ro brought her up to see me in the afternoon.... funny seeing her arriving at the door in a wheelchair. Thankfully, she looked fine and was quite chipper. We had a chuckle about how she was downstairs and I was upstairs, but we were in the same building tonight. Ro is going to sleep beside her so it's good to know she will not be alone. Her dad has been in and also Alice has seen her too – plenty of company, love and support. Although it pains me that I cannot be the one taking care of her, I am also extremely grateful to have such a wonderful family who continually rally round to support me at this time.

Mum told me she had been so worried it would all be too much for me because of how weak I was due to the recent operation, but thankfully all is well. It was such a relief to see Katy this afternoon to know that she is fine and well cared for.

23rd August

Katy was discharged; she was fine all night with no further complications, so that's brilliant news.

My friend popped in at lunchtime. I was delighted because I had just consumed my sixth chip as she came in. I said delightedly, "I've just eaten six chips," which was very quickly followed by an 'urge' causing her to speedily hand me a sick bowl. "Sorry," I said.

I had a lovely chat with one of my favourite nurses, Christine. It's going to be my thirtieth birthday in a couple of weeks. It's an odd thought to think that I could so easily not have been here to celebrate it.

29th August

My stitches have been removed. I was not prepared for what I was about to see. Due to my ignorance I had no idea about the size of the piece of my thigh that they had used to create the 'flap' to cover the hole in my stomach. I imagined something small and had not comprehended fully how the operation would work. Initially, all I could see was this huge missing piece of thigh that had now become this grotesque red blob on my abdomen. All I saw was more scarring!! As if I didn't have enough already!! I had imagined a small piece of my leg being put over a small hole in my tummy; the reality was an area bigger than the size of my hand, which had been moved from my thigh, and is now a red swollen-looking blob on my stomach.

I was devastated. I couldn't believe that I was even more scarred than before – shit! All I could do was cry. Mum was shocked as well. I don't think she had fully comprehended the extent of the operation either.

Generally, the surgeon is happy with the way it has taken. There is some bleeding under the tummy flap so they will take me to surgery tomorrow to ensure it is right. The surgeon has told me that while they are doing this, because the flap has taken so well, they will reduce it slightly. I feel relieved about this.

When they did the main operation they also attempted to graft my insteps. My left foot has taken well but my right foot has not taken, so it'll be a VAC dressing for my right foot. In general, the wounds on my feet seem to be healing well although both my heels are very sore with wounds. I cannot imagine what it will be like to stand on them. They are so delicate.

30th August - Shark bite

Today's operation went well and the surgeon is very happy. Having got over the initial shock of it I now understand why they took an area of such size. Firstly to make sure that it took; secondly, because it was a far bigger hole than I had imagined and thirdly, because they can only attach the flap that they created to 'real' skin, not grafted skin. Given the severity of the tissue loss, it meant it had to be attached to my real skin, which ends just below my belly button.

Although I understand and am coming to terms with it, I am gutted about the huge scar on my left thigh. It is nearly as far down as my knee. My dear friend Jayne came to visit me and said it looked like a shark bite. We did chuckle about this being a far cooler explanation for it.

1st September - Sitting up!

Following the success of the bowel operation it is time to get upright. The nurses and physiotherapist came this morning and prepared me by informing me that they were going to get me sitting in a chair today. They have also shown me a very supportive wheelchair that I can then use to get around. I am equally excited and petrified at this prospect. It means I can finally get out and about and see the world again, but I am petrified that my stomach will not hold.

As the momentous moment arrived I should have thought how awful it would be from the experience of the tilt table, but that had become a distant memory. It soon came flooding back as the overwhelming sensations coursed through me. All thoughts of my body vanished as the overwhelming sense of feeling faint kicked in. I thought I would pass out; it took all my concentration to breathe and remain conscious. The first attempt only resulted in me sitting up on the edge of the bed before I needed to lie down again. The second attempt resulted in me ending up in the chair.

Ruth was arriving and I so wanted her to see me sitting up – I was determined to do it. It was a wobbly fear-filled journey from bed to chair – odd how just a few inches can be such a challenge. I think nurses, physiotherapists and all hospital staff are amazing! As I touched down in the chair I felt such relief, I'd made it. I thought the sickeningly dizzy head would subside as I sat, but it didn't. I felt dizzier than ever; again, it took all my mental strength to remain upright. I was determined for Ruth to see me and she arrived just in time. She joined in my celebrations and delight about being out of bed, but struggled because I looked so awful that she just wanted to cry. I managed about ten minutes before it was all too much. I really needed to lie down or I was sure I would pass out.

It was a welcome relief to return to being horizontal. It didn't take long for the dizziness and nausea to subside and I felt elated to have achieved such a monumental milestone. I was up and out of bed!

Mum came up with the best incentive that came with an added dose of distraction and we were on to a winner. Mum was very chirpy as she arrived about how much easier it would be for me to be able to feed Martha sitting up. I'm so grateful to my mum and all the family for feigning enthusiasm at times when they felt heart-broken and were struggling themselves. It *was* the perfect incentive and it worked. Shifting focus from myself and the dizzy symptoms towards Martha really helped and made it all the more bearable.

2nd September

More sitting today, I have been up and in the chair three times. Each time it has got a little easier. I sat in the wheelchair the second time and I was really excited about going to explore the hospital. Ro and I only made it to the end of the first corridor though before I'd had enough and needed to return to bed. Each time I can sit a little longer, however, it is definitely getting easier and my dizzy head is gradually subsiding.

And the other major milestone that happened was taking a few steps. Things seem to be changing thick and fast at the moment. Getting my mobility back is truly a fantastic milestone. The physiotherapist has given me a zimmer frame. I never imagined myself needing a zimmer frame (they're for elderly people) or a wheelchair for that matter. I am so grateful for all these devices that are helping me to regain some independence and begin to move around again. I was really worried about my feet being too painful to walk on, but although challenging and uncomfortable, it is not unbearable. This is such a huge relief for me. I've still got the VAC dressing on my right foot, so I have to carry the pump around in a bag. It's a little cumbersome but not too bad. I often think how things could be so much worse and that seems to keep me going. I managed to shuffle a few steps to the door and back; it was completely exhausting but another cause for celebration.

3rd September

I had the most amazing gift. After I fed Martha I was chattering away when her face suddenly lit up in the most amazing smile. The first smile I had received. It makes me well up just remembering it. Thc joy that coursed through me was ecstasy; I haven't experienced that feeling for months! Mum said it was her first smile ever. I am over the moon to receive the first smile. I'm not sure if it really is the first ever smile but it doesn't matter. It's still so special. I never doubted I would bond with Martha because of the bonds I have with Katy and Amy, but it has been very sad for me to miss out on the initial days and months of her life. Prior to her birth I had been so looking forward to breastfeeding because I had loved it with the other two; such a special thing that only Mummy does. Not to mention all the other caring duties with lots of cuddles and getting to push the pram. Still, at least I had the first smile today AND I could so easily have not been here at all and never known her. I have time for this now and I am truly grateful.

I also managed to walk out into the corridor. I can't believe the amount of effort and concentration that it takes, not to mention how just walking a short distance feels – like I have run a marathon! Still, it's further than yesterday and each day I feel a little stronger than the day before. What was also glorious was I got to go to the toilet on a proper toilet. A moment of dignity and independence! Well, mild independence considering that I need someone to help me get upright and out of bed in order to be able to achieve it, but a start nonetheless.

The other 'adventure' was that Ro and I visited the canteen with me in the wheelchair. It was quite overwhelming to see so many people and the hustle and bustle of day-to-day life. We didn't manage to stay too long but it is yet again another 'first' and another milestone on this long road of recovery.

4th September - The shower

"Are you ready?" the nurse chirped. "It will be lovely to have a nice shower."

It had been eleven weeks since I had had a shower or bath. Part of me was really looking forward to it and part of me was really worried. This would be the first time that I would be seeing my 'new' body in its entirety. A scary prospect, as I didn't like the little bits I'd already seen.

The nurse wheeled me down the corridor and into the shower cubicle. She helped me remove the gown and move onto the chair she had already placed in the shower.

It's traumatic enough to see the wounded and mutilated body of another; it is quite something else to see the wounded and mutilated body of yourself! As I looked down, it was unrecognisable to me. I knew it would be bad but it looked worse than I had expected. It looked hideous from top to toe! I had thought I was prepared, ready to see what I was left to deal with from this devastatingly destructive disease, but I was so wrong. I met first with horror and shock. I look like some sort of freak. Like one of the people you'd see in a freak show back in Victorian times. All I could see was this mismatch of flesh – all of it angry, red and puffy. The piece of leg that had been placed over my stomach to cover the hole was still huge despite being reduced. The huge wound on my left thigh, as well as the red scars all around both my thighs (the remnants of the donor areas), blackened toe tips, scars all over my feet and around my ankles, healing holes in my legs, even the piece of remaining flesh on my stomach that was still mine, had a long red scar line on it from the bowel operation. I hate it, I hate my body. I don't want this body. I looked down at myself and despair washed over and through me like a creeping darkness. So much so that I felt my temperature rising. It is all too much, I cannot deal with this. My head began to swim. "Are you alright?" the nurse asked, as I passed out.

I woke to a right kafuffle going on around me. I could hear the sound of running feet in the corridor and the nurse was speaking to me, reassuring me that everything was okay and that I'd be back lying down in my room very shortly. The words swam in my mind, 'everything is okay,' 'everything is okay,' but everything is NOT okay. I look hideous! I've never been 100% comfortable in my skin but 'that was okay' because I looked normal. Now I just look weird. How can I ever feel even remotely happy with myself again? How can I ever feel comfortable with my body now that I look like this? I WILL NEVER, EVER BE HAPPY AGAIN!

The nurse was covering me in a towel and then I heard Kevin's calm voice, "It's all okay, Wendy, we've got your bed here and we're going to get you onto it and back to your room." Those same words, 'it's all okay.' I wanted to scream, "NO, IT ISN'T. IT IS FAR FROM OKAY!" but I couldn't speak. I could hardly breathe as the fear and panic coursed through me, giving it everything they had, just like the winning horse in a race as it charges for the finish line. As its nose passed the line and the immense pace finally slowed something else began to arise from deep within. As they lifted me onto my bed I collapsed into deep sobs. I thought of Ro; how could he ever love me properly like this? We will never make love again like we used to. We will never combine like one again. I have been deluding myself that we will return to normality but we never will. I used to adore the way he would kiss my body from top to toe, the way he'd move gently from my breasts over my stomach to those oh-so pleasurable places. Now that would never happen again. The thoughts swam in my mind, pulling me deeper and deeper into their infinite dark pool of despair. Loss, grief and loneliness drawing me in like a siren luring my body and mind into a fatal lethargy, draining all hope in the process and leaving an empty vessel in their wake. For a brief moment I did not want to go on, the pain was too great to bear. And then an angel appeared in the form of my mum who serendipitously arrived onto the ward at the exact same moment that I was being wheeled down the corridor and back to my room. She ran to me, took my hand and kissed me on the forehead. The nurses wheeled me into my room and my mum held me while I sobbed and sobbed. "I look hideous," I stammered. We both wept, until eventually the tears subsided.

Sometimes there is nothing that can be said or done to make something better. Sometimes we just need to allow the depths of our sorrow to be felt and expressed because nothing can make it better or take away the pain. Yet, somehow in our allowing, we find peace again and the strength to carry on.

5th September

The revelation is that tomorrow I get to go home for the day to see how I get on. I can't quite believe it. I will be turning thirty-years-old tomorrow, a key marker for anyone but a doubly auspicious event for me! I hadn't thought about going home yet and had anticipated it would be a while yet, but I'm really glad. It has taken all my focus away from my worries and despair and instead moved my attention to the children and home life.

The osteopaths have visited and they are organising lots of things to help me at home. We have three steps up to our house so they are going to erect some bars to help me, an extra handrail on the stairs inside and various other things. These things will be a seat for the kitchen so I can sit and prepare food or cook, and a commode, as we do not have a downstairs toilet. I'm not keen on the idea of this, but I don't have the strength to go up and down the stairs so I don't really have a choice. Mum informs me that she and Ro have moved a bed downstairs in case I need to sleep and lie down.

I have also now been given crutches so that I can get up and down the stairs and have been trained in using them. The incentive was... if you can't do it, you can't go home. I was determined! My feet are not too bad if I don't stand for too long, but my thighs are a real challenge. After a short while of standing this awful burning and itching sensation happens in them. I think it's linked to the donor areas and I wonder if it's something to do with all the nerve endings coming back to life. Having to deal with the blood circulating more could also be a contributing factor. I did manage the stairs through gritted teeth and passed the test! I cannot wait for the morning to come.

6th September - Two milestones in one day!

6:30 am

It's my birthday, thirty today! AND I have the best birthday present ever because for the first time in three months I get to be at home. Visiting for the day... what a gift! It feels like an age has passed since I've been home. I've got the now familiar mix of emotions that comes with each next step, scared but also really excited. The ambulance people are coming at ten am to transport me home and will pick me up again later to bring me back. I can't wait to see the girls. Mum and Ro have organised for them to be there as well. It will be so lovely to be with them, to be able to see them ALL day. Their visits here are always so short because it's boring for them. I have missed them so much. I can't wait to cuddle and hold them, to watch them play. I feel so excited right now that for the first time in ages I actually feel like I have energy. I'm not sure how it will pan out throughout the day but I'm not going to dwell on that.

Christine has just been in and given me a lovely card. She wrote, 'You made it' in it. I did indeed make it. It's odd to think how easily I may not have seen this day, not been here. Yet here I am waking in a hospital bed with the exciting thought of being in my own home very soon. Ten am seems an age away! I can't wait for Ro to come in. Let's enjoy good old toast and cereal to while away the time.

7:00 pm

I have had the most incredible day. It was so lovely to be home, to sit on the sofa in our lounge, to hear the girls playing and laughing, to see Martha so much. I loved it. My beautiful friends Jayne and Paul came to visit. It was the most perfect day. Ro bought me these two amazing pictures; they are incredible prints of lovers entwined. I love them. Mum was really concerned that they were inappropriate given the state of my body because they are virtually full-length bodies, but I know the sentiment and feeling beyond the visual image. Today my hope returned as I can see the love in Ro's eyes. He makes me feel so happy and it was so wonderful to be with the girls. To see my three beautiful daughters in their home where we should all be. Today I am glad to be alive. I will make it through this.

Margaret next door sent over a chocolate cake for me. I couldn't eat any though. I did try but it was too rich. It's so hard to eat right now, the doctors want me to eat loads of calories but I struggle to even eat a morsel of anything. Rich, calorific things are the worst as they just make me feel sick. I find those prescribed milkshakes, which are full of 'good stuff', a serious challenge. My weight has always been on my radar. Maybe I will never have to watch my weight again – that would be a bonus. I have always loved food and I've always had a goal of nine stone, but have fluctuated between ten and eleven stone for as long as I can remember. Which reminds me, Ruth really made me laugh in ITU one day with a story from when I was sedated. The doctors asked for photographs of me prior to being ill; they were keen to see what I looked like normally. That explained the photographs on the wall that I had thought were boxes of babies' booties. The doctors said this could really help with recovery. They had also asked what my usual weight was and she had told them that I was usually nine stone. At that moment I looked a long way from this, having not only post-pregnancy weight, but also being very bloated and swollen from my body's attempts to combat the toxins. They had responded with a very surprised, "REALLY?!" to which she replied, "No, not really... but if you could send her out like that she'd be very happy."

Anyway, onto the best news of the day – I'm going home tomorrow for good! I am super excited, I can't believe it. I never expected that I would be allowed to. When I arrived back Christine said to me, "I didn't expect you to come back." I studied her and then said, "Can I? Can I go home for good?" She went off and returned quickly with a huge smile on her face. "Yes, you can," she grinned. I can't believe it and I can't wait. Hurry up tomorrow, I'm outta here!

Chapter 5
Home

7th September

I can't believe that finally I am going home. It's been such a long time. It's kind of funny to be going home with a zimmer frame! I'm so weak it's astounding so I'm a little scared, but also feel excited. For such a long time going home has been the goal, yet now that the goal is here it seems like the beginning of another long stage. I don't think I'd thought about what was next once I got home, just going home. A bit like having a baby where the pregnancy is all about the birth, then suddenly you have a baby to look after and you've not really thought past the pregnancy. Anyway, it will be lovely to be in my own home environment again, to be with Martha all day and the girls are coming home as well.

Ro has returned to work full time now, but we are so lucky because Mum is able to stay with us. She has been amazing and told me yesterday not to worry. She will stay for as long as I need her. I cannot thank her enough.

3:00 pm

Well I'm home. It's lovely. I hope I can make it upstairs tonight to bed. I am determined to. I want to sleep next to Ro and not downstairs by myself.

8th September

Well, I did make it to bed upstairs. There was a moment where I didn't think I would. As I stood at the bottom of the stairs it all seemed too much and I burst into tears thinking that I wouldn't make it. My body is weak, my feet are incredibly tender and I had not walked very far at all, only shuffling to the commode and back. The stairs appeared tantamount to climbing a mountain and the summit seemed miles away.

Ro was brilliant. "Come on," he said firmly yet encouragingly. "You can do this." He has been amazing throughout. I can't begin to imagine what it must have been like for him; the fear of losing me forever, then the constant drain of being my carer, champion and supporter. I know that I have leaned on him completely; he is the one I always want near me and he was the hand that brought me back. As I mentioned before, I really don't know what I'd do without him. Somehow he always manages to say the right thing to give me the strength to carry on, even when I feel that all strength has left me. I will never be able to thank him enough for all that he has done for me; seen and unseen. There are no words that will ever compensate for it. Thank you Darling, you are my rock.

I'm still waking regularly throughout the night to wee. Not only is this a pain but it is also tiring. I feel a bit bad because I have to wake Ro to help me get up and onto the commode each time, so it's breaking up his night's sleep as well. I really hope this pattern settles down soon and that weeing once again becomes a daily activity and not a night-time one.

I woke quite a few times due to the springs of our mattress; they are quite obvious and were uncomfortable on my sides. My ribs are very close to the surface now and there is little padding due to the loss of tissue. Ro has put some extra padding on top of the mattress today, which hopefully will make it more comfortable for me.

Mum has Martha in with her and is undertaking the night feed. We did discuss having Martha with Ro and I but decided the most sensible option was for Mum to have her, as Ro has enough going on looking after me in the night let alone Martha as well. Part of me is sad but I know it's the right thing and at least I get to see her all day now. She had a bath tonight. Mum has bought this special tub that's a bit like a see-through bucket. She got it so that I could be part of the bath experience as it means we can bathe Martha in the living room. I love it and Martha appears to love it too. She looks so cute in it, it makes me very happy.

Katy and Amy have returned home as well. It's so wonderful to have my whole family together and to be with them all. I think we have a long road ahead, but as long as we are all together, life will be fine. I am glad to be alive.

9th September

Katy and Amy are so amazing. I thought it would be ages before they saw my whole body. My left thigh and feet are bandaged but you can see the scarring on my lower legs and they have seen this. I thought it would be a long time before they saw my torso, but as I was getting dressed this morning they both came in to see me. "Can we have a look at your body?" Katy asked. I'm not sure if they had been talking to each other about it. "Okay," I agreed, a little apprehensively I must admit. I really didn't want to frighten them or for them to feel so terrible about it like I did myself. The memories of the shower incident were not too far from my mind.

The girls were sort of fascinated by it. They both gingerly touched my sides where the grafted skin is. "It's okay," I said, "It doesn't hurt." I am still astounded by just how well they took it. They saw pretty much all of it. Then it wasn't long before that was 'boring' and they asked what we were going to do today. I love them for this. For helping me to get it in perspective and realise that life goes on.

10th September

My top news to report is that I only woke once last night to go for a wee. I am so relieved. It is the best night's sleep I have had since being ill!

14th September

I have had a few challenges with my digestion. Firstly, it was constipation but now it's mostly some sort of irritable bowel syndrome. It's very unpleasant and often leaves me needing to lie down and deep breathe through the cramping pains and sweats. This is hardly surprising though and I am just grateful that at least my bowel is functioning by itself. Although terribly painful when it happens the spasms do not last too long and settle down within twenty minutes or so.

Mum and I seem to have settled into some sort of routine, which I find comforting. Ro is at work in the day and Mum takes Katy and Amy to school in the morning with Martha. I'm very tired and don't seem to be able to rouse myself till around eleven am. She then helps me get up, washed, dressed and downstairs to the sofa. Then I play with Martha while she gets me something to eat. We watch TV in the afternoon while Martha sleeps, before Mum goes to pick up the girls from school. They come home, we watch TV, play a little, then Ro's home and it's dinner, bath and bed for the girls. Then it's not too long before I'm ready for bed myself. I'm sleeping well now, which is great.

Most days seem to follow this pattern unless we have a trip to the hospital.

25th September

We went into the hospital for dressing changes on my feet. I still have the VAC dressing on my right foot and it seems this will be there for a while longer. They have measured me for some special pressure garments that will help all my scarring to flatten out and look better. The garments will be ready in a few days. The first ones are knee-length leggings and a vest top that zips up the front. Once the bandages come off my feet they will also make me special socks. I don't really want them because I want to feel normal and these feel like something else which is not normal and certainly not attractive, but I will wear them because I hope they will help.

29th September

I received my pressure garments. It's a bit of a palaver to get into them and they want me to wear them all the time, day and night. I find them quite comforting for my stomach. I did have this stretchy, supportive band that fastened with Velcro, but it used to ride up a little. The shorts of the pressure garments come right up to my waist and so 'hold' everything in and feel very comforting. The daily massage of the grafted skin seems to be helping. I hope that these new garments will help to flatten out some of the wedges that exist where the grafted skin meets my normal flesh.

I bashed my ribs on a door handle. Not very hard but it nearly sent me through the roof!!

We follow a similar daily routine and I'm growing stronger each day. Not surprisingly, I still need lots of rest and tire quickly.

Ro continues to be my rock and I miss him when he's at work. Mum has been great, Martha is doing fantastically and Katy and Amy seem fine as well. Ruth has also been wonderfully supportive checking in with me regularly. She's an amazing source of emotional support.

October

I continue to get stronger and am beginning to get out and about a bit more too. So far it's just been the necessary hospital visits, but now there are some more day-to-day things like shopping. It's great that the big stores have wheelchairs so I can borrow one. I still cannot walk very far because of my feet.

One of my biggest secret fears has been about being physically intimate with Ro. I wanted to be close to him but have also been feeling really scared about this. Partly the physical aspects and also how I look now. Ro has continued to obviously love me, to give me kisses and affection in cuddles.

When I had my last check-up I asked the plastic surgeon whether it was safe for me to have sex. He explained that it was fine and should not be a problem at all. I'm very glad to say that 'physically' he was correct. The first time we were both very afraid but it was okay. Emotionally, with how I feel about myself, it's a different challenge. I don't feel desirable at all, in fact I feel downright ugly, plus my body is still very delicate. However, we managed to find a way and I can still orgasm. What a relief!

The pressure garments are far from sexy and as I am supposed to wear them continuously day and night, it doesn't really put me in the mood. Still, at least everything works physically, so that's a good place to start. I hope we can find some sort of return to how we were prior to all of this. This was always a wonderful, nourishing and fun part of our relationship.

The VAC dressing finally ended on the twenty-sixth, which makes getting around a little less cumbersome. I now do not have to worry about the pipe or bag. My feet are still bandaged though and are incredibly delicate. I have wounds on the outer edges of both heels, which still look far from healing I have to say, and one of my toe tips is still black. The doctors have said they will operate soon to remove this toe tip and make it more comfortable.

November

The surgeon operated on the fifth to remove that final black toe tip and trim the bone so that the wound could heal and close. It healed well. This meant it was time to think about some shoes as I had been wearing some blue hospital Velcro shoes all this time. I had no idea what sort of shoes to wear! I used to love shoes, not in an Imelda Marcos way, but they always finished off an outfit for me. I always loved the femininity of a heeled shoe. Like so many other things, those days are gone as well. I am now totally flat-footed and have limited movement in my toes. In addition, I get a whole load of pain if any pressure is applied to my toes. This means I cannot push my foot into a shoe. I managed to get some special shoes made that offer good support and are also easy to put on as the laces undo really low down. They're not very attractive but they are practical, which is just what I need right now.

This month I have been plagued by dreams of being pregnant. Usually the realisation of the reality of my situation enters the dream in some way. Sometimes I know that I need to have a Caesarean section because I cannot give birth, yet even in the dream state the pregnancy is still happening and all will end well. Sometimes the reality filters in enough so as to not make it too distressing, yet other times I wake and burst into tears. The depths of sadness are gripping me like a vice. I find seeing pregnant women really difficult and there is a heavy sense of grief that I was unable to breastfeed Martha. I feel like so many things have been taken away from me. I feel robbed of so much that I had been looking forward to, something quite normal like caring for your newborn child and the joy of your new growing family unit. I fantasise about a surrogate baby so that I can at least breastfeed it. I read somewhere once that you can induce breast milk in women.

In the end I went to see my GP because it was getting too distressing. He referred me for some counselling. I just had four sessions but it has really helped. I had attributed all this to being ill after having Martha and therefore triggering memories of a huge period of loss, grief and trauma in my life. When I told the counsellor that I was struggling with seeing pregnant women she said, "Well, you would, having lost your womb." It was like she switched on a light. I had not thought of it that way at all, but it made total sense.

I had always wanted four children. Now that would never happen because I had no womb and therefore no way to have the other child I had always dreamed of. I had attempted to console myself with the fact that I was so lucky to have three beautiful girls, but of course the thing to let go of was my dream of four children. Sometimes letting go of a deep desire and childhood dream takes a little more than a justification from the mind.

I still get very tired and find it difficult to get up in the mornings, so Mum will be with us for a little while yet. She is so wonderfully supportive and is happy to stay as long as we need her. I don't want to rush into her going and then wish she could come back.

I can't believe that Christmas is on the horizon already.

December

The really positive thing from this month is that I can now drive again – it feels amazing!! It is so wonderful to have my independence back, finally. I still can't walk very far, but being able to drive is brilliant. I have a disabled badge, which is really helpful. It means I can park close to things and therefore minimise walking. It means I can now take the girls to school *and* pick them up. I don't like driving too far at the moment but it's great to potter around my locality.

Mum and I have had the final hospital visit for dressings. It has now been agreed that a district nurse can do them for me at home. What a fitting end to the year. I've made great progress this month and feel ready to look after my family again. I know it's time to release Mum and let her return to her own life. Mum is delighted that I have made such great progress, although also a little worried about whether I can really manage everything without her. I think I'm ready and we have decided that she will return home just after Christmas. This means we can all enjoy a fresh start for the New Year.

January–March 2002

The early part of the year has gone well. I have adjusted to being independent and looking after the girls. It's been okay and it feels really great to be getting back to some sort of normal family life. The really exciting news is we have found a new house and will be moving in April. It is nearer to a park for the girls and is away from the main road, so I think it will be much better for them with their bikes and scooters.

April 2002

The move went really well and we love our new home. We now have three flights of stairs, which is probably not that sensible but is actually good exercise. The great thing about being here is that it has brought another layer of independent mobility for me. Well, semi-independent with the aid of electronics! The sunshine this month made me long to be outside by taking a nice walk. There's a gorgeous park and gardens down the road and I wanted to be able to wander down there with the girls.

I've always been one to look for solutions and thought there must be a way. This was when I had the idea to get a wheelchair. I tried a manual one at first but I wasn't strong enough for this. You really need to use your torso to propel yourself along and my weak stomach, coupled with Martha on my lap, made this really hard. It exhausted me just to get round the corner. However, this was quickly replaced by an electric one, which was made possible by the house move. The steps we had before would have made it impossible, but now we have a garage and so I can store the wheelchair in there. Perfect.

On the first run I stormed down the driveway and nearly revved right into the road. Chuckling to myself, enjoying my new-found freedom with fresh air on my face, I set off round the corner. This is where I discovered the challenge of the camber. As I was motoring along, there was a camber in the pavement because of a driveway. I wasn't sure how to approach this but thought I would make it and kept going. I slowed down but the chair spun round and lurched onto the road. I nearly hit a parked car! Only my hands prevented a disaster. Surprisingly I burst out laughing, probably from shock! I had to get out and shove the chair back onto the pavement before I could continue. Mum was dreadfully worried by this story, whereas Ruth loved it and laughed till she cried!

I have discovered that I need to plan my routes to find the low curbs to cross roads. We've quickly adapted for the school run and local shopping trips, and with Martha strapped on my lap it works really well.

Katy and Amy love it. I tend to drive them to school in the mornings and then go in the wheelchair to pick them up. They ride on the chair across the playing fields; Katy stands on the back and Amy sits on the arm. We bomb over the playing field at 'top speed.' (Okay, not that fast, admittedly, but fun nonetheless). Good times!

I've even managed to master that tricky camber which nearly had me on the first trip out. I worked out that if I drive at it at full pelt and steer very slightly towards the right, I could take it. (I rode motorbikes as a kid).

The other excitement this month is that we bought two gorgeous kittens. I've never paid for pedigree cats in the past but my friend had two of this breed and I absolutely loved them for their coats. They're Burmese and feel like velvet to the touch.

I've got this sense that where I am going next is not tactile – when we die, I mean. I think this realisation arose from the near death experience, from that moment when I was aware of myself but not in my body. So in some way it feels like a real gift to be able to touch and feel in our material world.

I love stroking the cats, they're super soft. We have a boy and a girl. I actually intended to just buy her, as she's what they call a blue, which is a fabulous grey colour. When I got there he was such a cute tabby I couldn't resist him as well. Their names are Sapphire and Cosmo.

As I am now able to do the dressings myself, the district nurse is now visiting infrequently to check on me. This is really wonderful and it has marked another moment of independence as I can now shower all by myself! I have had to use the bath up till now, with both feet elevated so that they stay dry. It's been a bit tricky getting in and out with me needing some help from Mum or Ro. Now though, it is so lovely to have a shower, to be able to wash all of my body. A shower is so much more refreshing than a bath and the main thing is of course the total independence of being able to do it all myself. I can see why small children get such joy as their independence blossoms. Utter bliss!

May 2002 - Making it pretty

The time has come for some reconstructive surgery and I met with my new surgeon. The initial plastic surgeon has left but I have never forgotten that he said there was a lot they could do to make it all look much better. I remembered he had said that I would end up with a scar like a smile on my tummy. What they are going to do is implant balloons under my good skin, gradually expand the skin over time and then remove the scar tissue. They will then use the expanded skin to cover the scar area. This will result in me having line scars rather than large grafted areas, which I think will help me feel much more normal.

The new surgeon seems really nice and has suggested we start with my leg. It is time to repair the shark bite!

5th June

Today has been hard; in fact the last few weeks have been hard. As Amy and Martha's birthdays have approached, so has the anniversary of being ill. This has resulted in mixed feelings for me;

excitement for Martha's first birthday and Amy's sixth one, but equally sadness about all the devastation that happened to us this time last year. I have found myself feeling very sad and crying frequently. It's a bit like being back there in some odd way, haunted by memories that I would rather forget.

On the whole, today has been lovely. Martha is so cute it's hard for her not to put a smile on my face and warm my heart. Amy has had a lovely day as well. So really it's all good; I just wish I wasn't plagued by this recurring sadness.

June–October

On 17th June the reconstructive surgery for my leg began. The surgeon implanted three balloons in my left leg underneath my normal skin. This was followed by weekly visits to the hospital where they injected a small amount of fluid into the balloons to expand them. This went on for four months until the skin was sufficiently stretched to cover the scar. It was an odd experience and I managed to hide my expanding thigh underneath a wraparound skirt, so it wasn't too obvious.

On the whole, the experience went fairly smoothly. There was one day in August, however, when we took the children to the park that was not so great. The balloons were quite large by this point; three bulges on my thigh, each about the size of a large orange. It was a glorious sunny day and everyone was having such a lovely time. As I followed Martha over to the sandpit I tripped on a piece of edging sticking up and fell forwards. Fear shot through me as I was so worried that I would burst one or even all of the balloons and it would all have been for nothing. As I landed on the floor, shock paralysed me for a moment before I burst into tears. Ro rushed over and helped me to sit up. Luckily, the balloons were all fine in my leg. I didn't actually fall on any of them. My knee was pretty sore but I rapidly became aware of what other people would think of this blubbing woman. It took a while for me to stop crying because I was really shaken up. It's funny how you can think that you are fine and dealing well with something, yet the reality is that you are on the edge of constant vulnerability. It doesn't take much to push you over the edge.

Thankfully, there weren't any other challenges to my fragility and the operation was 90% successful. There was still a small area where the surgeon stretched some skin across that hadn't been expanded; a couple of days later this area split open and so I had to have a small graft on this area. The rest of it joined together quite nicely and left me with a line scar rather than the previous grafts. They did look a lot better and I was very pleased with the results.

November 2002

Feeling encouraged by the success of reconstructive surgery on my thigh, albeit a little apprehensive at the idea and practicality of having expanding balloons in my back, I was keen to go ahead with further reconstructive surgery. Unfortunately, when I met with the surgeon to discuss the next phase he was not so keen. In fact, he really didn't want to do it. "I'm concerned," he said. "The grafted skin is so close to your bowel that I am worried your bowel will be affected if we try to remove the grafts."

"I see," I said, trying to take it in. Although I was initially disappointed, it made sense and I really didn't want to cause myself further complications by having bowel problems. I left the appointment feeling a bit dazed. This was not how I had expected it to go.

Gradually, it began to sink in as I was on my way home. This was it. This was what I was left to live with. This was as good as it got. My mood grew sadder by the minute. I just managed to make it home; I was in total emotional turmoil. I didn't know what to do with myself. I wanted to die. I couldn't imagine ever being happy with myself, with the way my body looked. As soon as I got in the door I rang Ruth. I could hardly speak, "Please... help.... me," I managed to get the words out before breaking down into sobs. Ruth was amazing, as always. She, like Ro, always manages to say just the right thing. Even though she didn't know what was the matter she started saying the right things. Eventually, I managed to tell her what had happened and what I was so devastated about. Typically, Ruth was really positive as she tried to convince me that I *would* feel sexy again and I *would* be happy again. Somehow she triggered a little ray of hope within me. By the end of the phone call I was still sad but no longer completely in despair. Ruth had somehow given me a glimmer of hope and it was enough to give me the strength to keep going. So this was it. This was how I would look for the rest of my life.

In that moment it felt like I had been given the whole picture in bite-size pieces. I am pretty sure that the idea that there was much reconstructive surgery that could be done to improve the appearance of my body had given me the will I initially needed to carry on. Because of this so-called knowledge I did not give up in the early days. I did, of course, have the option of finding another surgeon who would do the operations, but for me, the risk outweighed what was, in truth, a superficial outcome. I don't mean shallow; I know that how we look has a powerful influence over how we feel, more that the idea of my bowel not functioning properly and having to have a colostomy bag seemed worse than what I currently had to deal with. This left me with the task of learning to love and accept my body just as it was. Something that I really couldn't imagine ever happening.

Chapter 6
A New Dawn

2003

I don't really know why at the time, but I got drawn to Eastern philosophy for my healing. This opened up the world of energy in my body and the world itself. To me, it's very real because I have a direct experience of it. The first experience came in January 2003 when I began practising Tai Chi and Chi Kung. I was honoured to come across an Oriental teacher who was well connected with his own energy and was passionate about awakening it in his students as well. I was performing a Chi Kung exercise when I suddenly felt this strong buzzing sensation in my hands and arms, as strong as if you were to hold a mobile phone in your hands that was vibrating. "What the fuck?" I thought. After calming down, I realised that it was *my* energy. I could not believe that I had been ignorant to it for 30 years!

March saw the end of the wheelchair. I was really delighted by my progress and that only one year later I felt strong enough to walk to school and back. I told Katy and Amy with great delight that I no longer needed the wheelchair. They made me laugh because they were really disappointed. Nothing to do with me, simply the fact that they now had to walk home instead of hitching a ride!

I continued with the Chi Kung and Tai Chi because I discovered it was really helping me to become even stronger. I decided I would look into training in acupuncture to find out more about this mysterious world of energy. I began researching where I could study, but I couldn't find a course that fitted with the family. Then serendipitously I went to visit the mother of an ex-boyfriend who had visited me in hospital and told me to come and see her. Her other son happened to pop in and was really pleased to see me. He updated me on his family and asked me what I was up to. I mentioned the acupuncture and he told me that his wife had studied Shiatsu. I'd never heard of it but he told me it was a bit like acupuncture but without the needles. That sounded good to me; I still didn't like needles! He also gave me her number and told me to give her a call, saying that she'd love to hear from me. I gave her a call later that afternoon and thoroughly enjoyed catching up. Edina had also experienced ill health that had resulted in looking at alternative remedies herself. She'd done some really interesting things and was also now into meditation. She added that her and a group of friends had been praying for me and sending healing energy when they had heard I was ill. That made my heart melt, to think that people from the past and people I didn't even know were thinking of me. She offered me some healing and invited me to join a meditation group that she held. I happily accepted both. Edina also told me more about Shiatsu, which sounded really interesting. There was a school in Devon, which offered taster days, so I arranged to attend one.

I had been reading and researching Near Death Experiences (NDE). The term seemed to be used for a variety of different experiences. Some people were physically in trouble but didn't experience anything beyond their physical reality, more that the fragility of their life became very apparent. Others had experienced some sort of out-of-body state where they were looking down on their body with a deep sense of peace. Others reported experiences of things similar to mine. They were the presence of light, peace and love, including something beyond our usual perception of material reality. Some of the reports were incredible such as people experiencing profound insights into life beyond our physical form.

Psychology has always fascinated me and I had been reading some psychological literature about NDEs. One of the theories is that an NDE is something that happens in the brain at that point and is therefore, nothing mystical. I began to wonder if this was true. My NDE was so vivid and real at the time and also when I reflected on it. It seemed more like a memory than a dream, but perhaps it wasn't any more real than any other dream. I also knew that I was medicated at the time, so I wondered if that had triggered the experience too, perhaps. I began to dismiss the NDE as some sort of brain phenomenon.

In the summer I went on a Tai Chi weekend workshop. Ruth was with me, and our group walked to Wistman's Wood on Dartmoor. Wistman's Wood is a phenomenally beautiful spot, with gnarled, stunted oaks and an abundance of mosses and lichens. On arriving we were asked to sit in silence and eat our lunch. I have to say initially, it was a painful experience as my head was so busy that I longed to talk. After some gesturing and silly faces with Ruth (I guess it took me back to being at school and not being allowed to speak!), I did settle and sat on a rock by myself. The rock was covered in mosses and it was really soft to sit on. I found myself examining the various lichens and mosses; they were so intricate and delicate. I suddenly realised how strong the moss was that I was sitting on.

When I got up, it would spring back up again, whereas if I *were* to have the proportionate weight on me, it would squash me. From this idea came the most fundamental respect, love and feeling of unity and 'oneness' with nature. I always knew that nature was alive, but I previously had this perception of nature and myself as two separate things. This experience really made me *feel* the life in nature and the 'oneness' of life and the knowledge arose that I was actually a part of nature.

We were next asked to choose a tree for an exercise. I duly found a tree and began the exercise. With my eyes closed and my palms towards the tree, I began to breathe gently and moved my hands slowly towards and away from the tree. All of a sudden I lost all sense of my separate self and experienced an overwhelming sense of peace and love. This was very similar to my feelings experienced during the NDE. I *knew* that Unconditional Love was the source of all life; everything came out from it and returned to it. It was a truly beautiful experience, a moment of absolute reverence before this thought arose in my mind – 'peace and love, man!' It made me laugh to myself about the hippies in the 60s and my awareness returned to my separate self.

This experience confirmed two things for me: Firstly, it was another direct experience that there is something greater than myself, than this separate body and personality called Wendy. Some sort of Universal Source of energy, light, wisdom, God; call it what you will, and this greater thing *is* Love. Not the contracted love that has conditions to it, but an expanded all-encompassing, non-judgemental Love. Secondly, it is that **life is spiritual because there is no separation**. Within each of us is an inner yearning for unity, whether we are aware of it or not. It is our natural state and we somehow have this idea and belief that we are separate. That is why the way we currently live in separateness causes us so much pain.

A few weeks after this Tai Chi weekend experience I awoke very awake around five am with a sentence in my head. I turned over and tried to go back to sleep, but the sentence was on a repeat loop and would not stop. After a while I decided to get up and write it down. I was wide-awake and there seemed no point just lying there tossing and turning. I got out of bed, put on my dressing gown and went downstairs. I turned on the computer, opened a blank document and began to type the line that was in my head. As I began to type, the first line was replaced by another line, and on it went. It was like taking some sort of inner dictation, and I just kept writing until the sentences stopped. I wrote for four hours straight, not stopping once as the thread of information poured into my mind and onto the page. I wish I could tell you that I could share it with you now, but in ignorance I didn't fully understand it back then, and didn't look after it properly. It got lost somewhere along the way. I can, however, tell you the core message, which is that fundamentally, there is fear and love and everything else comes in between. As humans we have a choice of where we reside and whichever we choose creates the life we experience. The choice is ours, but it is important that we choose love. It was a strange experience, this stream of words that seemed to appear in my mind. It was like a manual for living, inviting me to be more loving and open. Some of it was quite blunt about how we live and the pain we cause to ourselves and to others. It was difficult to hear but it was equally making complete sense. Some of it was like a step too far for me. One line I will never ever forget was 'All is perfect in God's plan.' That line really freaked me out. I didn't believe in God and I certainly didn't believe it/He had a plan. However, it did seem like wonderful wisdom. I made a vow to learn and understand what it meant, to live more fully in love rather than fear. Little did I know then the huge commitment that I had made and the journey that was to follow.

The Shiatsu taster day was fantastic in two ways; one: It was wonderful for my body and two: the theory had me intellectually intrigued. I joined the course, which was three years of training beginning in September. I was enjoying sitting in the meditation circle and this new exploration of spirituality.

I kept a journal of my thoughts and ideas. One day while I was writing, I found myself drawing a circle with Unity at the top and Separation at the bottom, with arrows suggesting an on-going flow. This was a complete eureka moment! It was obvious to me that this was life. Unity to Separation and back again, on and on and on; every human lifetime was a cycle, and also the collective greater human history. I got the sense that we were on a return journey as a species. We had been to the brink of separation and were returning to unity. I was so excited that I jumped up and interrupted Ro who was programming. "Look!" I said excitedly. "This is it. This is life. Unity to Separation and back again."

My mind was buzzing, yet clear. I felt like I'd just been given the most precious piece of insight. 'This must have been how Einstein felt,' I thought, with his revelations.

Ro stopped what he was doing, looked at it and just remarked, "That's lovely," then immediately returned to what he had been doing.

I couldn't believe that he wasn't more interested in the secret wisdom of life. Oh well. He had been very busy on his computer spending long hours attempting to create an online business.

Obviously I was a little deflated but went back to what I was doing, writing and pondering. I suddenly wondered why I was here. Why did I come back? What was the point of it all?

I wrote it down as a question… 'Why am I here?'

Immediately in my thoughts the wisdom responded... 'You are here to help alleviate the suffering of mankind.'

I put down my pen. Shit! 'How am I going to do that?' I thought. That seems like an insurmountable task and I have no idea where to start. I'm still suffering, myself; I don't see right now how I can help anyone else.

Chapter 7
Work of Art

2004

Ro was tapping away on the computer as usual. It was late. "Hey you. I'm going to bed. Are you coming?" I asked with a little wink. You know, the one that couples do in a 'nudge, nudge, wink, wink' kind of way. I was trying to keep some mystery to it rather than just saying, "Hey, shall we have sex?"

"Okay. I'll be down in a second. I'll just finish this," he replied.

As I mentioned, he was trying to get an Internet business started. He worked long hours on it and seemed to lose all track of time while he was doing so. I got into bed and waited and waited and waited. This was a familiar pattern and one that pained me deeply. I looked at the clock and one hour had passed. I'd already been upstairs again to see if he was coming to bed and met the same response of, "I'll be there in a minute," yet he still hadn't come to bed. I felt so desperately sad. I so needed to be held and loved.

During the day, Ro was still intimate with me and would kiss and hug me, however, it was very infrequent that we made love. The nights had become more awkward and painful for me. I think Ro is repulsed by my naked body and so I ask the 'nudge, nudge, wink, wink' question less and know I have begun to withdraw from him. It is so painful when he rejects me that I'd rather not ask at all.

In the meantime my body is healing well. The lumps and bumps are smoothing out, the reddening is fading, but I feel ugly and freak-like. I feel robbed of my physical body, my strength and my womanhood but, worse than this, I have lost my connection with

Ro. I miss what we had. I miss him so much. It is devastating. We don't really talk about it and I don't know what to say. I don't want to know how difficult he finds it. I don't think I could handle that. I feel so sad and I don't know what to do. I cannot hold back the tears any longer as they well up from inside and overflow silently down my face. I have cried so much over these last few years I am surprised that there are any tears left!

During these frustrating times I was finding solace in my exploration of spirituality. I was somehow trying to make sense of the equally strange and wonderful experiences that took me beyond my normal experience of what life was. One particular book connected me with a group of like-minded souls and Ro and I went away for the weekend to attend a gathering. On the first evening this guy kept catching my eye. I felt like I knew him. I could feel him looking at me from across the room. When I'd sneak a peek he'd smile then look away. I was curious, and to be honest, enjoying the flirtation. It felt good to be getting attention.

Finally he came over and introduced himself. He was very confident and self-assured with a beaming smile. I instantly really liked him. The main draw was his talk of energy and our creative capacity as human beings to use this energy to manifest and create our world. I was totally hooked and wanted to know more. I really enjoyed being around him that weekend. I felt a strong sense of connection between us.

A few months later in the year I attended another gathering and wondered whether he would be there. This time I went on my own, as it was not Ro's thing. My heart skipped a beat as I walked into the room and there he was. "Well, look who it is," he said, with a grin.

Throughout the evening he had the whole room captivated with his stories and insights. He had a set of crystals that he used a lot and really commanded the space. The evening was really good fun, it was great to be with such an open group and we had a really good laugh. I was thoroughly enjoying myself. As the night wore on I got the chance to talk to this intriguing man more. I was hooked. It was like something was waking up inside me. Throughout the rest of the weekend we flirted a lot. It was a real boost for me to feel fancied. I felt sexy and like a woman, something I had thought I would never feel again. I told him about what had happened to me, about my scarring and this didn't seem to put him off at all. I had the urge to show him my torso, testing to see if he would be repelled. I revealed a little of my side and he was very kind and gentle. Far from being repelled he said it was amazing.

I can't tell you how much I needed to have that response. Ro's physical distance was destroying me. I really thought that he was repulsed by my physical body now and couldn't bear it. This was my explanation of all the nights when he didn't come to bed; a wounded mind trying to make sense of a reality that it couldn't comprehend. Little did I know at the time that I couldn't have been further from the truth.

As the weekend drew to a close I was sad to leave. I had felt the best I had for a long time. There is nothing like a bit of sexual attraction and attention to boost one's energy. The attraction between us was very strong but, like me, he was also married and so I didn't think anything would come of it.

When I returned home we began to e-mail each other. This started infrequently at first, but it very quickly became daily. I enjoyed the banter, exploration and flirtation. I felt amazing for the first time in a long while.

We continued to e-mail lots of times throughout the next few months. Then the next group meeting came around. I couldn't wait to see him again. We arranged to meet the night before. I was really nervous and to be honest, more than a little torn. There were the morals of my marriage; my love for Ro, my children and my intrigue with this man all lumped in together.

He talked a lot about presence and about there only being now. He talked a lot about human codes of agreement and how there was no right and wrong, only the rules and limits that we place on ourselves. I took this information and shut out my churning feelings of guilt about Ro.

When I arrived at the hotel I was nervous and excited. We had a glass of wine and chatted for a bit. When we went up to the room I had some doubts. What would he think of my body? Would he be repulsed? What about Ro? What about the kids?

I pushed all these thoughts out of my mind and let myself concentrate on the feelings of my physical body. What happened next was perfect for me and just what I needed. As we lay naked on the bed he ran his hand over my torso, then moved back to look at the whole thing. "Wow," he said. "It's like a work of art! It reminds me of that lovely statue that's made up of layers." He went on to explain about the statue, where it was and what it was like, but I wasn't really listening. 'A work of art, a work of art,' I kept thinking it. Now that's a new way of seeing it. It was like music to my ears and honey for my heart. I so needed to hear that sentiment that day.

After a wonderful weekend where I had deliberately blocked out all thoughts of Ro and instead ridden on a wave of passionate attraction, I began the journey home. Nagging guilt feelings began to intrude but I pushed them out of my mind by focusing solely on the present moment. The colour of the cars, the trees and anything else I could focus my attention on other than the fact that I had been unfaithful. When I arrived home I felt a bit awkward but did my best to push all thoughts of the weekend from my mind. I almost convinced myself that nothing had happened; that perhaps it was a one-off and that was all it was.

We continued to e-mail each other and inevitably the whole thing immediately intensified. He had his own business and we started to think about whether I could work for him in London so that we could see each other more. I couldn't see how this was feasibly possible. I had the three girls at home and couldn't leave them in the week. I liked the idea of it though, not just because of him but it felt exciting to be pondering the many possibilities of going back out into the world of work again. What he was doing sounded exciting. I was fascinated by the idea of the power of the mind to create our reality. I was desperate to know more and I couldn't get enough of this sort of information. I wanted to control my life and to make amazing and extraordinary things happen.

Then I had an e-mail from Katy and Amy's dad. He said that he and his wife would like to have the girls to live with them full-time when Katy started secondary school. He suggested a swap so that I would become the weekend parent. This was totally unexpected and I wondered whether it was the universe nudging me in the direction of London. I have always been one to think outside the box and so didn't have the belief that as the children's mother I had more right to them than him. I knew we both loved them equally and rationalised that they had been with me for seven years, and so it only seemed fair that they have some time with him.

I spoke to Ro about it, but not really properly; in hindsight it was more like I informed him rather than discussed it with him – for my bloody-mindedness, I am so sorry. I spoke to the girls. Again, the gift of hindsight would have been good. I wanted to know what they wanted to do. They were very rational and said the same thing I had thought about, having lived with me for the last seven years and so why not live with Dad? That's what we decided to do. In the summer before Katy started senior school, her and Amy would move to live with their dad, his wife and their stepsister.

I continued to e-mail this man and fantasised about this tremendously exciting life that I could lead. I was desperate to see him again. Eventually we fabricated a business meeting so that we could spend the day and night together. Ro was okay with it and I was all set to meet him the next day. That night Ro went out and I had a highly flirty and sexual conversation on 'live chat' with my mystery man. Ro was very late back and so I went to bed.

I got woken in the early hours by something landing on my stomach and Ro demanding, "How long has it been going on?" He walked out of the room. My stomach sank, as it dawned on me that he had printed out the conversation from earlier that evening. 'Oh God,' I groaned internally; that conversation had been really sexual and I felt dreadful that Ro had read it. Not because of being found out but because of how painful it would have been for him. I would have been utterly devastated if the roles had been reversed. Crikey, you couldn't write a better soap opera script... Imagine it... the audience knows that Ro has set Wendy's computer to record all online conversations. As Ro goes out for the night they are watching, wondering, 'Will she use the computer tonight or will she phone?' Then, not only is she on the computer but it is a seriously saucy conversation as well. Yikes! In that moment, I decided just to be completely honest. I took a deep breath and went downstairs to the kitchen where Ro was sitting at the table.

The whole thing was extremely civilised and a bit surreal really. I made us both a cup of tea and we very calmly talked. He decided to move out the next day and we went to separate bedrooms that night. I wanted to see some emotion; I wanted him to fight for me, to know that he cared. I didn't think he was that bothered given the lack of... well anything, really. How could he be so calm? Perhaps he was relieved in some way and I had done him a favour. Right at this moment I'm so confused and do not understand him at all. I thought we had something special that could never be broken, yet here it is – broken.

That night I was in shock. I couldn't quite get my head around everything. It's like when that 'on the shelf' fantasy suddenly bursts forth into your reality and you begin to wonder if you really want it at all. The thing you really want is about to walk out the door and it's your entire fault. I was the one that had made my world implode and was powerless to stop the metaphorical walls from crashing in around me. Finally no tears, I just felt numb. Needless to say, I cancelled my meeting the next day. Ro moved out to his mum's and I did my best to continue to maintain some sort of stability for the girls.

The mystery man turned from a man of excitement into a total pain in the ass. He was far from supportive and instead seemed like another demand when I had nothing to give. A couple of weeks after Ro left I was driving in the car when he rang. I didn't answer because I was driving and it rang off. He immediately rang back again. I managed to pull over and answer the phone. What with trying to get myself together and look after the kids, this was a pressure I could do without. I told him where I was at and that I needed space, not to be hounded. He said it wasn't enough. "That's fine," I replied. "Then it's over." As I hung up the phone, the relief flooded through me just moments before the reality hit of, 'Oh god, what had I done?' I'd hurt Ro, ruined my marriage and torn my family apart. And for what? Some stupid silly illusion created by my mind. The mystery man had talked a lot about love, but what I saw in that moment was a lot of ego, a lot of judgement, supposition and superiority. I thought to myself, 'Ro has more love in his little finger than you do in your entire being.' And as for me, what does that say? What an idiot I am. Here I was attempting to live in a more loving way with greater awareness and yet all I'd done was create a whole load of unwanted drama, pain and angst.

I felt really sad about Ro. In fact, devastated is more the right word. I really did love him very deeply, and after everything we'd been through and having little Martha together, it seemed such a shame. I chose not to die because I didn't want to leave him and yet here I was really miserable, deeply sad and just about functioning, having destroyed the one thing I wanted by being unfaithful. It seemed so ludicrous. I was consumed by misery and did not know what to do with myself. To make matters worse he has moved into a house share with a so-called female friend of mine who suddenly seems not to be my friend. I thought I would feel better once we parted but I feel terrible. I feel consumed by jealousy wondering what they are doing. I'm sure she fancies him as she is even offering to help with Martha when she visits him. I feel so awful. What is wrong with me? It's my fault and I have no right to say anything about what he does with his life, but I can't bear it. I miss him so much; he consumes all of my thoughts.

In this despair, Eckhart Tolle's wonderful book *The Power of Now* landed in my hands. Thank you Eckhart, you may have saved my life! This book taught me the experience of presence. Far from using the present moment to be free of consequences (what goes around comes around; what you give out you get back; as you sow, so shall you reap... Let's face it, Karma is real and you can't escape it); the experience of presence is one of peace and bliss, no matter what the external circumstances, as I was about to discover.

After weeks of moping around and feeling sorry for myself I started reading *The Power of Now* and was enjoying it. I went into the kitchen to get a cup of tea and suddenly realised I felt happy. It was like a miracle. 'Bloody hell, I'm happy,' I thought. I really relished the feeling because it had been absent for such a long time. It didn't last long though and soon I lost the experience of presence and was once again consumed by the antics of my mind. However, it had given me a glimpse of something else, a moment of respite amongst my self-imposed mental torture.

A few months later Ro came back. We both missed each other dreadfully and were both miserable without each other, so we decided to give it another go. He was very forgiving and simply said he loved me. I didn't know how he could do it. How he could be so forgiving. I still felt bad about it. We did our best to get on with life as usual, but sadly the next few months revealed that nothing had changed and we still had the same problems that we did before. I still felt so disconnected from him and it pained me deeply. I missed him so much and yet he was right in front of me. Here we were back in the same pattern of him on the computer till all hours and me feeling lost and alone. I could not tolerate it. It was like each day it consumed more of my thoughts and became a bigger problem. It felt like it was sucking the life out of me. I didn't know what to do about it. For some sad reason we just did not work.

In July 2004 we decided to separate again. As the girls were moving to Bath in August I decided that I would move to Bristol so that I would be twenty minutes away from them (which would make it possible to see them in the week for tea). The idea of being solely a weekend parent seemed too sad, but with a visit in the week I thought perhaps it could work. When the girls moved in the summer, I moved out as well. It was an odd day. I had hired a van and Ro helped me load it all. That same undeniable chemistry was there between us and a huge part of me didn't want to leave. It took all of my focus not to cry as I drove away.

Martha and I began to settle into our new home. Mum was only twenty minutes away, which was lovely and it brought us closer to Ruth as well. As planned, we began seeing Katy and Amy for tea in the week and they seemed to be settling in well. Their stepmother had created a busy itinerary, getting them involved in lots of after school activities. I needed to have an operation on my right foot to correct the bunion in my big toe. This had been causing me a lot of pain and I was hopeful that walking would become more comfortable following the surgery. Sadly, this meant that I would not see Katy and Amy for tea in the week for a while, as I wouldn't be able to drive for eight weeks. We would still manage the weekends, thanks to Mum. Ro came to visit and stayed over, to see Martha and the girls. It was really strange to have him sleeping in the house. I still had a huge draw to him and I used to really look forward to him coming. Part of me really wanted to see him, to spend time with him, but it was also painful at the same time. What a strange situation we were in.

Things never seem to work out as I think they will. The experience of something is often different to the projected thought I had about it. The operation on my foot was a big success and it healed really well. Although the downside was eight weeks of settling into a normal routine for the girls, resulted in them deciding that they no longer wished to do the weekly tea visit with me as they were so busy in the week. My weekly visit got cancelled. This meant I ended up seeing them less than I thought - letting go of Katy and Amy was the hardest thing I have ever done. I missed them dreadfully.

I was in the final year of my Shiatsu Diploma and began to get closer to Dave, one of my male friends from the course. We began to chat and share more. He was lots of fun and we laughed a great deal. He was also very open emotionally and I really enjoyed this. I liked exploring and having deep conversations. Our friendship evolved and we started having an intimate relationship.

Ro was still coming and staying for the weekend to see Martha; I thought it was best to let him know that I had started seeing someone rather than him hear it from Martha. It was all a little uncomfortable and awkward as I informed him that I had started seeing someone. He just went completely silent. He sat for a long while before going to bed. Again, I wanted him to fight for me, to show me something. He didn't show any emotion and just left as soon as he could the next day.

I continued to see Dave; it was a very nourishing relationship. At the end of my six months tenancy, Martha and I moved over the bridge into Wales to be closer to Ruth and her family. Martha was close with her cousins and I thought it would be nice for her to have the company. Also, it was not too far from Katy and Amy. I thought I was over Ro. I knew I still cared very deeply for him, but that was okay. One weekend I got a real shock.

It was February 2006 and it had been Valentine's Day the week before. I had a Shiatsu training weekend in Devon and took Martha to Ro's for the weekend. I couldn't help but notice a Valentine card on his mantelpiece. As I realised what it was I felt my stomach lurch. I felt sick and jealousy gnawed away at my insides. I knew he had been doing some online dating and had started looking for someone. This made me feel sick too, even though I tried to be upbeat and chatty about it. Boy, this was confusing. I went to my Shiatsu weekend. Seeing Dave made everything even more confusing.

After the weekend I collected Martha and headed home. The hour and a half drive up the motorway was an ordeal; the feelings of jealousy, guilt and self-punishment were overwhelming. I felt terrible inside, so deeply pained; I didn't know what to do with myself. It felt like being torn apart from the inside out. No morphine on offer this time to escape the emotional pain by drifting into a drug-induced sleep. What to do? What to do? In the end I stopped and bought a bottle of wine and a packet of cigarettes (god bless the old crutches). I got home, settled Martha in bed, got a glass of wine, a cigarette and went outside.

I took a drag on the cigarette and having not smoked for a while it totally spun my head out. I felt dizzy, stumbled backwards and sat down with a bounce on Martha's little trampoline, at the same time simultaneously pouring wine all over myself, and promptly burst into tears. What a crazy, unnecessary mess I had created.

I had a difficult and fitful sleep that night, but in the morning some rational thought had returned. I knew I had to let go. I loved Ro but I knew it didn't work and all I wanted was for him to be happy. I felt bad about the pain I had caused him. I also felt selfish about taking Martha away from him and wished that there were something I could do to make it right. That day I sent Ro a bunch of mixed roses with a message... 'Mixed roses for my mixed emotions. I hope you find the happiness you deserve.' I really thought there was no chance for us and that he would not be remotely interested in being with me given the number of times I had hurt him so deeply. This was plighted by the fact that I had also since been with Dave as well. I can honestly say that I didn't send them as a 'get back with me' plea, it was much more of an 'I'm really sorry for hurting you. I wish you love and happiness because you deserve it.'

I didn't expect to hear anything from Ro and was really surprised when I received a text from him saying, 'What does that mean?' I explained about my confusion and he said he'd come and see me. I was totally honest with Dave and shared that I was not in a good place to be having a relationship with him because I couldn't give myself up fully to it. I knew it wasn't fair to be with him if I was still in love with Ro, and so we ended our intimate relationship. He was amazing about it and we continued to communicate as friends.

When Ro came to see me he told me he had never stopped loving me and wanted to get back with me. I was so worried about messing it up again or it not working again and he said, "I'd take five minutes with you if it was all I could have." And so we got back together again. We were all really happy. Katy and Amy were really pleased, as were all the family and obviously it was wonderful for Martha to have her dad with her every day. When the Welsh six-month tenancy came up for renewal we decided to move further into the countryside and found a lovely country residence near Hereford. We got a puppy, started a vegetable garden and all was well.

What a cliché, talk about trying to create what I imagined was the perfect life! Needless to say, it wasn't long before country life lost its appeal and that nagging sense of something missing returned. I decided that I would focus on studying. I'd always wanted to do a psychology degree and I earned a place at Exeter University. In March 2007 we moved back to Exeter. It felt like coming home and I really enjoyed being back and catching up with friends. What I was struggling with was that Ro and I seemed to be slap back in the same situation of disconnection. He had begun to build a DJ business, but this meant that he was away for lots of weekends. When he was home he spent long hours on his computer. Inside me the same nagging, ugly beast of discontentment began again with its incessant moan.

I tried everything I could but my discontent grew. We kept having 'chats' and yet we never seemed to get anywhere. Ro would often say we were going round in circles and I have to agree that we were. I was desperate to make it right, to rekindle what I felt we had lost, but I felt powerless to change anything. Where was the connection? It was like a drug, like the best quality cocaine that coursed through my system lifting me to the highest heights, yet it only brought me crashing back down to the depths of the lowest lows. I couldn't get my fix, I just couldn't find it, yet that lack of connection consumed my waking hours and I couldn't bear it.

Another external catalyst showed up in the appeal of another man towards whom I felt utterly drawn to. I did not want to be unfaithful and so confessed to Ro about my desire for this man and we separated again. The new guy was an absolute disaster. It was a total whirlwind fortnight of deep trauma and personal growth before, yet again, I wondered what the hell I had done. What a total twat!

In that couple of weeks, Ro met another woman. I was devastated. I dissolved into deep pain and, yet again, didn't know what to do with myself. I was so angry at life, at myself, at him, at her, at the unfairness of it all. This was coupled with a suffocating sadness that infused me to my very core.

Ro was staying at his mum's and there was a moment of uncertainty for him. I begged him to not give up on us and I longed for him to choose me over her. I knew he was pondering which way to go, and as I clicked to open the e-mail from him my stomach was churning. I don't remember all the detail but basically it said, 'I am moving in with Ruby and once we are settled we could maybe have Martha to live with us.'

I couldn't believe it. Moving in with her? After two weeks!? One thing for sure was there was no way I was letting Martha go. I'd made that mistake already with Katy and Amy and I was not going to make it again. I pulled myself together as best I could and focused on Martha. The anger and jealousy were horrible. It was consuming me like a hideous beast eating me up from the inside.

The next time he came to pick up Martha, Ruby was with him. I couldn't stand it. It was like someone had flicked a switch and turned on Anger. I managed to be civil and hold my tongue, but my reception must have seemed like the sub-zero temperatures of the Antarctic! Ro had a sports car that he really loved and as they drove away I felt so angry I wanted to take a hammer and smash it. I found it hard to contain my surging anger. What to do? What to do? I was physically shaking with it. I texted Ruth…

'He just turned up to pick up Martha with HER! I'm so angry. I could smash his stupid fucking car with a hammer.'

A moment later my phone beeped…

From Ro: 'I take it that text was not meant for me.'

Oh god! I'd only sent that text to him. Shit! I burst into tears. I would never have really taken a hammer to his car. Did he now think I was some crazy psycho bitch? Sobbing, I went into the kitchen and leaned on the side. That's when the bowl sitting innocently on the drainer from the crockery that was 'his set' when we met, caught my eye. The anger surged again and I picked it up and smashed in on the floor. Phew! It felt good. The floodgates opened along with the cupboard that contained the rest of the set of crockery; I smashed the lot!!

I was so angry. Love stinks!!! It's all bullshit. The rest of that day I went round the house and found all the gifts of love he had given me, all reminders of him, anything and everything I could find I destroyed. The beautiful pictures of love, gifted to me on my 30th birthday and return home I removed from the frames and tore to shreds before burning the pieces. I was a mess! That night I collapsed into bed and sobbed till I eventually drifted off to sleep. Now though, the anger was at myself. What had I done?

The next few months were tough. I did my best to contain myself but it was really hard. One weekend with Katy and Amy I got annoyed about the absolute state of their bedroom. For some reason they seemed to have got out every toy and game they could find and it was all over the floor, quite literally. After I'd initially ranted about how ridiculous it was and why couldn't they be tidier, I began picking things up. Amy sheepishly came in and was helping pick things up too. The first tear rolled down my cheek and I could no longer contain my sadness. I sobbed and sobbed and I couldn't stop. Bless Amy, she said, "I'll pick it up, Mum. Please stop crying." "I'm so sorry," I sobbed. "I can't stop." Sometimes our pot is full and the only solution is release.

Sometimes as adults, we are so laden with other stuff; we must be quite hard for kids to fathom. I felt sad for them. I was no fun. Each time Martha visited Ro and Ruby she would return with various gifts that *She* had given her. I managed to keep my mouth shut but I'm ashamed to say that often those gifts would quickly disappear. I couldn't stand the visual reminders of something that I did not want to think about. One day as he handed me the new bits Ruby had given Martha I said, "Do you have any salt with those?"

The Universe decided to add its own salt too. Number plates had just switched to the new style of 00 and in our area this got coupled with an 'R' on many plates. This meant his name was everywhere! 'R0' repeatedly jumped out at me on every single bloody car journey! Then as another little side dish of salt, the radio regularly blared "Ruby, Ruby, Ruby, Ruby!" Thanks, Keiser Chiefs!

July 2007 brought a wonderful change. Amy came back! She hadn't been getting on well at her dad's and wanted to live with me. It was ironic that I had just managed to finally accept that they had gone and would probably never live with me again, when I received the phone call to ask if she could come back. I was delighted and so was Martha. Katy chose to stay in Bath, as she was very settled with a lovely group of friends.

It was lovely to have Amy back. She really took my focus and it all became about getting her settled into her new school, with me starting at university and our united family unit of me, Amy and Martha settling into a rhythm. Time to buck myself up. Time to stop being mad at myself and angry at the world and instead begin to build a new life.

Chapter 8
Oneness

"You've got to come and try this," my wonderful friend Edina said. "Funny coincidence, because I'd heard about it twice and then the hairdresser mentioned it as well. You know I'm not one to ignore such coincidences," she laughed.

"What is it?" I asked, intrigued.

"It's called Deeksha," she replied. "It's a channelling of energy to calm the mind and help awaken us to Oneness." (It's now known as Oneness Blessing).

"Sounds lovely," I said. "I could seriously do with that right now, my mind won't shut up!"

I agreed to join her so she gave me the day, time and address of the next meeting. I arrived at the house and didn't know what to expect. It was a very normal looking house in a normal looking street, which was a good start. I also had faith in my friend to not lead me into some weird cult. A very friendly lady welcomed me in and I sat down in the circle, which was a small gathering of about ten people. She explained that all I needed to do was sit and relax and they would come round and place their hands gently on our heads about three times. The first time it happened it felt nice and I relaxed a little more; however, after the second time silent tears fell down my face. It was a new experience for me because there was no sob, no thought about why and no tightness in the back of my throat. This wasn't like my usual experience of crying, but simply tears falling down my face. It felt kind of nice and so I didn't resist it. Afterwards I felt really peaceful and my mind was totally quiet. No barrage of Ro-related tragedy story to maintain the current of inner turmoil and self-punishment; simply peace, simply quiet. Bloody gorgeous! My mind remained quiet for a couple of days before the churning thoughts began to return. Because of these, I went to receive more Deeksha.

A few weeks later I saw Edina. "Come to Scotland with me?" she asked. "There is a five-day Deeksha intensive retreat. I bet it will be amazing. Do you fancy it?"

It didn't take a moment's pondering for me to know that I really wanted to go with her and experience the intensive. If the transformative effect of the short evening sessions were anything to go by, it would indeed be amazing. "I'd love to," I replied with a smile.

Prior to being allowed to attend the retreat, a full form needed to be completed with details of my history. This included a disclaimer to be signed; it basically said that if I went mad, I had no grounds to sue. This sure did make me wonder what I was letting myself in for, but my instincts were yelling GO!

When Edina and I arrived at Penninghame House in Scotland we were immediately separated into different rooms. This annoyed me but I went along with it. The first gathering set the rules of being in silence for the retreat bar, speaking to the therapist or sharing in the group only when asked. I was initially really resistant to the silence and I wondered how we would deal with issues without speaking about them. The therapist, an incredible woman with amazing intuition and insight, asked us one question. "What are you feeling right now?"

It's a brilliant question because, have you ever noticed just how much you live from your thoughts in either the past or the future? It made me realise just how little I was simply fully present to what was happening right now.

I began to notice many other things too. Mainly just how insightful it was to shut up! I've always been one for analysis, with a thirst to discuss, to understand and make sense of things. I'd always looked outside for the answers to my problems instead of inside. I had always blamed others or the world for things not right in my life, even though I thought I was taking responsibility. Oh, how we can delude ourselves. I found it really difficult initially to start really connecting with what was inside of me. At the beginning of being quiet it was like my own internal soap opera... just as noisy as actually speaking to someone else. Analysis, questions, answers; all those little voices inside having their say. There was the voice of reason, the voice of conscience, the voice of doubt, the voice of the little pixie who says, "Yeah, you know you shouldn't do that, but do it anyway." You know the ones. Well, I hope you do or you will probably be putting the book down now and thinking that I am insane!

After a while the voices began to quieten down and I noticed how I had a real urge to talk about what was going on inside. I was fascinated by the process and had a strong desire to discuss my thoughts about the issue I was dwelling on. I couldn't because I was in silence and I was not allowed to speak. Part of me wanted to rebel, to speak. Why should I stay quiet? I understood now why friends were separated in the bedrooms. The urge to speak was really strong and I started to think that this silence lark was ridiculous. Why should I do it? How could we possibly solve our challenges in life if we didn't discuss them? Could I find someone else to talk to? Why shouldn't I talk, it was a free country after all? Other such thoughts swam through my mind. I had made a commitment though and decided to stick to it, so I turned my attention instead to my body and my breathing. Trying my best to just let things be. I noticed that I felt terribly uncomfortable in my body. The tension was really quite unbearable for a while but I kept reminding myself to return my focus to my breath and away from the incessant internal mental analysis. When I focused on my breathing and my body, this brought with it emotion, and I did my best to allow that too, without resisting it. It was hard but I just kept practicing, kept bringing my attention back to the breath. Both the thoughts and the emotions were like waves in the ocean, building in momentum before peaking and crashing on the shore, rolling in till they petered out and then returned back to whence they came. Sometimes the ocean was turbulent and fierce and at other times it was quiet and gentle.

I started to see that the thoughts were a distraction from the emotion; when there was intense emotion they invaded by attempting to be the reason, to make sense and justify it or to claim its initiation. Yet, when I could be bold and dive right in, witnessing the feeling sensations fully without judgement or the desire to get rid of it or run away, sudden incredible insight would arise. Wow, finally a really intelligent voice. The insights brought with them a sense of knowing - profound joy and peace. Also, an amazing sense of release and relief, a sense of something far greater than the drama I had been caught up in. This insight and knowing arose time and time again. Astounding!

I had an amazing few days of getting out of the analysis and into my body and energy. I became increasingly peaceful and fascinated by being the watcher of what was arising rather than the thing itself. I noticed that when I observed sadness it naturally dissipated of its own accord and that when I allowed frustration and anger it also seemed to disappear and transform into something else all by itself. One day we were doing some dancing and I got really angry about my feet. I wanted to dance and run and play and be free and I couldn't because they hurt. The anger arose first and I went to leave the room. One of the assistants came with me and there were some padded mats in a side room. She asked me if I was okay and I told her that I was so angry about my feet. About how damaged they were, how unsightly they were and the pain and discomfort that they caused me. As I said this the anger moved to sadness and I began to cry. I kneeled down on the mat and buried my head in my hands. Then the anger surged again and I banged my feet on the mat. It felt really good. After a short while of this I came to rest, and all of a sudden my whole body was tingling; I felt truly alive. It was amazing! All anger and sadness was gone and all that remained was peace.

The next day saw an explosion in the room of creative and playful energy. It spread like a virus from one person to the next until the therapist said, "Oh for goodness' sake, will you all go outside and run it off!" The energy was beautiful; it felt to me like being a child again. We all ran outside laughing with some of us holding hands, just like a junior school playground. After a few minutes one of the assistants came out and announced, “Okay, tea break.” Everyone immediately stopped and began to head inside. I was gutted. I felt filled with joy and enthusiasm. I wanted to play and explore but I didn’t want to do it on my own. I looked around for someone else to ‘play’ with but they all now looked so serious, back to being adults. ‘Shall I stop too?’ I wondered. ‘Nope,’ was the response. ‘I will just have to play on my own.’ I spent a bliss-filled ten minutes skipping around on the grass and enjoying the sunshine on my face, before I finally stopped and headed back to the main room to join the others.

The final day was my birthday; funny how things seem to happen then. I had a weird dream in the night and felt a bit out of sorts that morning. My mind immediately began to ruminate on being ill and all that had entailed. By the time I reached the meeting room I was feeling really sad. The therapist asked me what was going on and I started to tell her about my illness and my odd night. Her harsh response was, “Well, you’ve been fine all week, so you can either mess it up now or see what you are doing!” I was shocked. How dare she? She had no idea what I had been through and all that my body had suffered. I was so angry BUT I had learned two vital life-changing lessons that week; 1) She was bloody good at what she did. I had witnessed a woman who arrived thinking she was going to die, and looking like she was going to die, return to life before my very eyes; and 2) If I shut up and didn’t get defensive I would get answers of real value from the inside. I said nothing but took a deep breath. “You okay?” she asked. “I’m just digesting,” I replied as I closed my eyes and thought, ‘What a bitch.’

She moved on to check in with the next couple of people before we began the moving meditation. It took a while for my mind to come back from the distracting thoughts about her being unkind and the horrendous physical journey that my body had had to endure. The thoughts of losing Ro, the love of my life and the unfairness of that also kept bubbling up. It took all my effort not to get consumed by any of these lines of rational enquiry that seemed perfectly just. I kept dragging my focus to my body, to my breath and as the thoughts of my predicament began to subside, this one clear thought arose... 'I'm a drama queen.' Its delivery was so soft that it made me laugh. It wasn't a criticism or a judgement, it was simply a fact. A way I had been being. I could see that I was addicted to drama and I was using it in an attempt to get attention. I felt I had received hardly any of the therapist's attention that week because I was doing so well and I now craved that attention. I wanted to be seen and noticed. Wow!

All the times that I had been a total drama queen about things began popping into my head. There is something so beautiful about the Deeksha energy that allowed me to see with soft vision. Instead of my usual eyes of punishment and criticism, it showed me myself with eyes of love. I couldn't help but laugh at myself, lost in my own drama running round and round in endless circles. It seemed really silly. It seemed like therein lay the choice for fear and contraction or love and expansion. I could choose my old story, the past, the illness, the loss and be miserable. Alternatively, I could choose the present moment, the window of opportunity that it presented, to allow joy and peace to fill my being. The decision was mine to make.

There was a moment where Edina and I came together and I exclaimed, "Oh my god, I'm a drama queen." She burst out laughing and agreed with, "Yes, you are."

That week I discovered that when you look with eyes of unconditional love you could see anything. You can see all the games of the ego, all the ways we attempt to maintain the separation, including our addiction to drama. You see all the crazy and clever antics of the intellect that keep us believing we are separate from each other. I know that if anyone had told me before that I was addicted to my plight and using it to get attention I would have been really offended. Yet in that moment it was crystal clear that I was choosing to be unhappy by dwelling in the past. Prior to that I did not realise that I had a choice. The emotions were unconsciously and powerfully strong and were ruling the show and resulting in a mind in negative turmoil. A never-ending, ceaseless spiral that was impossible to escape with the intellect.

And so, from a morning of impending doom I left that afternoon feeling like I had been reborn, excited to get home and see the girls and really looking forward to the beginning of my psychology degree.

Life goes on

Amy was settling into school, Martha was happy and I was enjoying getting back into studying. I suddenly had the thought to go to the hospital and get some of the pictures from when I was ill. It occurred to me that it would either be a further progression in the healing journey or one of the stupidest things I'd ever done. I decided to go and see Kevin from Abbey ward, as he had always been really friendly and helpful. I visited the ward, which was both a mix of strange and nice. Strange to be back where such struggle had occurred; places are triggers for memories so undoubtedly I was bombarded with those, yet it was also nice because I was making new memories. In this moment I was stronger and more vital. It was also nice to say 'hello' to a couple of the nurses I recognised and their reactions were really wonderful. They were delighted to see me looking so well. I asked if Kevin was around and one of the nurses asked me to wait and said she would go and tell him I was there. It was always a bit weird for me in the hospital because my case was well known and many of the nurses had seen me when I had no recollection of them at all. It wasn't long before Kevin appeared with a big grin. "It's great to see you, you look really well," he said, "How are you?"

"I'm good, thanks," I replied. "Single now. Ro and I split up." I'm not sure why that was the first thing out of my mouth, perhaps because he knew Ro as well.

"I'm divorced now," he said.

We chatted for a while longer and I had the sense that he liked me. I gave him my mobile number and he said he'd text me when he'd sorted out the photos. A few days later he texted me asking whether I'd like him to post or drop the photos round? I invited him to drop them round and we spent a couple of hours drinking tea and chatting. The time flew by and we had a really good laugh. We arranged to meet up with the kids for the day at an adventure park with the idea that it's always nice to have other single parents with kids to hang out with.

When he left I got Amy and Martha to bed before I fired up my laptop to have a look at the photos. As it turned out this was not a mistake at all, they were incredible. It made me realise just how far I had come. As I looked at the one taken with cadaveric skin, I wept at the miracle of being alive. How was it possible from such devastation? I felt truly blessed.

We met Kevin and his kids at the adventure park in the October half-term. The kids collected pumpkins; they all got on well and had a great day playing. The day passed really quickly with Kevin and I chatting loads; it was all very natural and easy and he was great fun. He left first, and as I was packing up to go back to my car, I realised that I had all the pumpkins. Then, just as I was getting back to my car my phone beeped with a message from him. A smile lit my face, he *likes* me, I thought and I have the pumpkins. 'That's a good excuse for him to pop over and pick them up,' I thought cheerily.

Kevin and I saw more and more of each other. It was nice because I didn't have the obstacle of my body to get over, as he knew exactly what it was like. I found out that he had been integrally involved in my care right from the beginning… he'd even grafted one of my sides! So to him, my body was nothing unexpected or gruesome; in fact it could only look better than it had done.

The girls and I moved to a smaller house nearer to the school so that Amy could walk to school herself and give her a bit more independence. I focused my attention to my course, which continued well. I was glad to leave the old house with all the memories of Ro and move somewhere fresh. I still thought about

Ro, but he was gone. I had to accept it and I was thoroughly enjoying the flourishing relationship with Kevin.

He told me lots of things that I didn't know about when I was ill and helped me put some other missing pieces together. I understood what had happened to me in a much deeper way and it seemed like even more of a miracle that I was alive.

A couple of months into our relationship we had a disagreement. My neediness raised its head and I overreacted about something, which compelled me to leave a stroppy phone message. He came to see me the next day, by which time I had calmed down and could see I had overreacted. He was really uncomfortable about it though and simply said after a while that he needed to go. He left, but I begged him to stay and burst into tears after he drove off. I texted him a couple of times but there was no reply.

I thought he would contact me after a couple of days but I heard nothing from him. I then sent a couple of messages but with no response. Initially the non-contact from Kevin was really painful. My thoughts were consumed with the whole thing. I mentally beat myself up every day and analysed and ran re-runs constantly in my head. Neediness is like a beast that consumes you and, in extreme cases, controls you. The trouble was that I had exams looming and simply did not have the time to fill my head up with the tragedy of yet another ended relationship. I went to the shops, bought some cigarettes and started smoking (back to the old emotional crutch and, more to the point, the tool to shove all my emotions down). It worked. It's an age-old strategy and I got on with focusing on my exams. It was a good distraction needing to cram so much information into my head.

I had promised myself that once the exams were over I would stop smoking and deal with it properly. This I duly did and I did my very best to take everything I had learned at the retreat in Scotland and put it to good practice. I practiced presence and allowing. It was painful and difficult at first, but with focus and non-resistance the pain subsided and I felt happy. I made myself a promise not to contact Kevin at all. I knew that if I did it would be out of neediness, even if it felt like it wasn't. I knew that if I had any inkling of wanting to hear back from him then it was based on need. I could see how I was really good at deluding myself by attempting to convince myself that I was actually communicating out of care and not of need. It was hard but I stuck to my guns. As the time passed I felt happier and happier. I learned that just because someone has appeared to leave, you could still feel loving and positive about him or her. This also helped with Ro because I still loved him deeply. I found that when I allowed my love for him with no need to have him with me it felt truly wonderful, whereas when I tried to convince myself that I did not love him it felt painful. During this period I learned a great deal, and I am so grateful to Kevin for giving me such a wonderful gift. I started to ponder and was open to the differences between men and women. I read *Men are From Mars and Women are From Venus*, and *Mars and Venus on a Date*; thank you John Gray. I read several of Barbara and Allan Pease's witty, insightful and light-hearted books about the differences between men and women, which really resonated with me. I began to see that, yes we are different but that is beautiful. I love learning new things and I began to embrace the idea that men were amazing and just different... not wrong, as I had previously thought!

It was at this point that Edina asked me if I wanted to go to India with her to the Oneness University. I knew I really wanted to go and so we booked our tickets for an Indian trip in April. Here we would do a seven-day silent retreat. I couldn't wait. Mum was going to have the girls and I was looking forward to going.

I passed my first set of exams and stayed immersed in my studies. I was thoroughly enjoying all that I was learning. Life was okay.

It was now March, two months after Kevin had left. I was meditating one day when the thought of him popped into my head. In the past when I had previously thought of him he always felt distant. I asked "where is Kevin is in relation to me?" and I was expecting the feeling to be distant. It was so close to me that it made me jump. It felt nice and I wondered whether it meant anything. I had a sense that he would come back to me but let that go. Attachment to a desire is a breeding ground for discontentment. That much I had learned in longing for Ro to return for months! The following Sunday it was Mothering Sunday and I was ironing when the idea to text Kevin popped into my mind. At first I pushed it away, but it was there again. I checked myself to see whether I felt the need for him to text back. I didn't think I did and so decided that I would text him and just say, 'Hi.' I sent a message to let him know I had passed my exams and that I hoped he was well. I pressed 'Send' and placed the phone down, continuing with the ironing. I really didn't expect him to text me back, so much so that when the phone beeped it made me jump. I really hadn't thought for one moment that he would reply. 'Happy Mothers' Day x,' the text read.

A soft smile met my lips as I replaced the phone down on the arm of the chair, determined not to text back and carried on ironing.

Later that afternoon I received another text from him asking how I was, which led to several other texts before we arranged to go out. We met a week later, both with the intention of taking things really slowly and not to get too involved. It was lovely to see him though and when he dropped me home he kissed me at the doorstep. All our reserved intentions went out of the window as we fell back into each other's arms.

April 2008 – Chennai

It was so exciting travelling to India. I loved the smells, the people, the colours and even the crazy driving. I'd never experienced anything like it. Edina and I had a night's stop in a hotel before attending the Oneness University Campus the following day. We both explored Chennai and ended up visiting a beautiful temple. It boasted a gorgeous tree standing in the centre with hundreds of tiny ribbons tied to it. Apparently this was a place where people asked for things and tied a ribbon in thanks. I particularly loved the jasmine that seemed to be available on every street in wonderful garlands; its divine aroma filling the air – truly heaven scent.

The next day we arrived on the campus and were taken to our UK ladies' dormitory, which consisted of ten single beds with a bathroom down the hallway. It was perfectly adequate, clean and functional. I chose a free bed and a wardrobe for my things, which were limited at that time, as my bag had not arrived yet. At the first gathering it was requested that we keep contact with family and the outside world to a minimum, with preferably no contact at all. This process is a journey into your inner world and obviously outside contact would be a distraction. I knew the request of silence for the course, so prior to departing the UK I had discussed this with Kevin and had agreed that I would not be contacting him once I started the process.

The process and work in Scotland had taught me both the power of silence and of allowing internal sensations and feelings without running away from them. It's so easy to wind up getting caught in the surface story of memories and thoughts, or the outside distractions of the world. I learned that when I was quiet, instead of either persisting with my story through thought/analysis or maintaining the energy by sharing with another, was the moment when peace could be found. It might be more accurate to say it is where peace resides. This was the place where profound liberating insight would arise out of the silence. I could see that I was caught up in a world of drama; where the victim in me thrived and survived on strong emotions like fear, guilt, shame and sadness. These emotions can be very difficult to be with, and in an attempt to escape and alleviate my suffering I would discuss my plight with others. The 'sound' idea we've all heard of is a problem shared is a problem halved, but I was beginning to see that this was all too often not the case at all. Instead, all I was doing was keeping the internal fire burning, sometimes adding small sticks and sometimes adding large logs. Initially, there was some small modicum of relief in sharing, but the truth was that the pain was still there inside. This is not to say that sometimes it is not helpful to speak to someone. Sharing with the right person can do wonders for us. The process of getting heard within our deepest places is powerfully liberating. However, what I was perceiving was that I spent much of my time going round and round in never-ending circles, not really finding any real solutions because I was looking for the answers outside of me, in the outside world but the real solutions were *in*side of me. The real solutions came about through the changing of my mind and expanding my awareness. The real solutions also came through Unconditional Love where the parts of my psyche that lurked in the shadows were brought into the light and then, rather than being punished, were instead seen with Love. They weren't wrong or bad, they were just aspects of the mind. Aspects that kept me held hostage all the while that I was judging and condemning them. However, when I looked with Unconditional Love by actually welcoming them, was unafraid and unashamed of them, they suddenly seemed beautiful. They became simply aspects of the psyche. The most profound shifts arrived when I embraced my addiction to drama, when I saw that this was the mode of functioning that I was operating in. It was then I realised that I had a choice, and if I wished to function in a different way I could; it was possible to live in a more peaceful way.

Gradually, through the practice of presence I had begun to find peace in the moment. This began to open my eyes to the fact that my happiness was not dependent on my outside circumstances. How could this possibly be the truth if one day they 'made' me unhappy but the next day, despite no change in external circumstances, I was happy? My continued practice of containing my emotions rather than projecting them had been both difficult and profound. It takes huge effort to change the habits of a lifetime. However, as I continued to discover the incredible insight that was gently revealed from the silent place, it spurred me on. I would go so far as to call it revelation; as for me the insights were transformational.

Often we are firefighting, running away from our emotions, yet when we stop fighting and listen instead, life has a perfect way of revealing our deepest hidden obstacles to the truth of our Being. We are all products of the past, shaped by our life experiences and all the beliefs that have been handed down through our heredity and society. Yet, each little box that I consider to be myself is not who I am at all. In order to be what I truly am I needed to give up everything that I *think* I am. The difficulty is that I think I am a lot of things. When we earnestly and truly desire peace we will find it, yet we will not find it by looking outside of ourselves at the material world. The peace that we are unconsciously seeking, like homing pigeons, is within. Yet the veil that blocks the truth, though flimsy, is persistent.

And so it was that I set out with good intentions to maintain my silence but only managed two days before the desire to make contact with Kevin was really strong. In the process we were examining relationships and how we look outside of ourselves for reassurance from our loved ones because of the very fact that we are insecure. I listened to these teachings about insecurity and neediness but considered that I had 'worked hard' on this aspect of myself during that period when I had heard nothing from Kevin for two whole months (a serious man cave visit). I embraced it as absolutely perfect because it showed me so much. You see, everyone plays the perfect part in your life for your own liberation. The trouble is it's easy to slap morals and judgements over the top and think that their behaviour is out of line. This in turn only serves for you to remain in the dark. When we absolutely choose peace and truth over everything else then we have no choice but to embrace new thoughts about ourselves and everyone else. Then we can let go of all our old stories, beliefs and patterns. You see, you are not a body, you are not that personality. No one has ever wronged you and you have neither done wrong yourself. You are whole, perfect, strong, powerful, loving, harmonious and happy.

You are SPIRIT. You are LOVE. For the extent of this transition that we are currently experiencing to become complete, we need to practice and remain alert because it is so easy to delude ourselves… as I was about to find out for myself.

We have many false beliefs that continue to live through the nature of our repetitive habitual thinking. You need to see the exercise and cultivation of your thoughts, mindfulness and mind watching as absolutely integral to your wellbeing. Only when you really grasp the importance of this will you apply the necessary mental effort to train your mind. See it like a garden, you must plant thought seeds of love, harmony and joy in order to flourish and grow. Thought seeds of anger, resentment and blame create contraction, disharmony and unrest. Self-containment and self-soothing is a challenging task. Sometimes the feelings are just too big and it feels like they will swallow us whole. In this case seek help. Find someone else who can rest with deep emotions and simply let them be. This is so that they can hold your hand while you rest with the depths of your despair, i.e. loneliness, sorrow and grief.

As you can see, I thought I had triumphed over my neediness and insecurity, but I was wrong.

It is quite amazing in personal development how we strive and 'work hard' to overcome our limitations. In this moment right now I am smiling as I write this because the truth is, there is no 'hard work,' only surrender. There is only a deep letting go as we remember… 'All is well.' I hope you haven't just thrown the book across the room in sheer frustration and yelled, "If it was as easy as that I would have done it!" I hear you. What I want you to know is when you return home, when you are connected to all that is, there is no 'work hard' to change anything because everything is beautiful just as it is. When you Love freely, unconditionally, aka without judgement, then you are free to choose. Free to experience whatever you wish. If you feel you are working hard to change an aspect of yourself, know that you are caught up in thought. I have been walking this path for such a long time and am still a work in progress. I'm still continuing to learn and grow but there is a state where we reside with Love as our companion and then everything becomes easier.

Anyway, back to the story – two days of no contact and the urge to text Kevin was strong. I had a little debate in my mind as to why I should or should not text. Eventually I decided that one little text would surely not hurt. When I got back to my bed that day I turned on my phone and was gutted to see that I had no reception. For a moment I lay on the bed disappointed, but then I got up and went to walk about, surely somewhere there would be reception. I eventually found it up on a roof and sent a message to Kevin. Later that evening I received a text back from him. It made me feel so happy.

The next day Edina said to me, "Please don't get cross with me, but I have to say this to you. Ask yourself why you feel the need to contact Kevin." It felt like I was being slapped, and I was instantly defensive before I shrugged and walked off. The internal discomfort was horrible. Initially I tried to escape via my thoughts, projecting it out onto Edina. 'Edina and her psychic abilities, she's always got something to say,' I thought, really pissed off! I instantly withdrew this thought, knowing that it must be something about myself for me to even feel pissed off. As it was still lunchtime I sauntered slowly to the meditation hall while having an inner debate with myself. I arrived at the hall twenty minutes before the next session was due to start. I slipped off my sandals and lay down on the ground. 'No time like the present,' I thought. I attempted to feel the discomfort, rather than avoid it with the mind games. I said a silent prayer, 'Please help me stay with this discomfort and show me the truth.' I started to breathe deeply by bringing all the attention to my churning solar plexus – then there it was... BAAM! I suddenly realised that I was insecure. It came in this sentence that I heard in my mind, 'Well, you've been insecure in every other relationship, why should this one be any different?' The thing was far from being a problem; the gentle truth of this statement was a huge relief, like I'd been hiding something in the dark while desperately hoping no one would see my secret. With my secret now out in the open I felt absolute joy and rapture. How I laughed and laughed! Every time I thought to myself, 'I'm insecure,' I would fall about laughing again. It seemed so funny, yet so beautiful - and not a problem at all. I realised the problem was in the denial of it, not the thing itself. I had this image of myself standing up in a group like in an AA (Alcoholics Anonymous) meeting and saying, "Hello, my name is Wendy and I'm insecure." With rapture and bliss wrapping me up, the root revealed itself. I realised that I did not love myself. I consistently battled and resisted this idea all afternoon. Previously, I had really believed that I *did* love myself; I'd done the affirmations, I'd cleared the emotional baggage and I had psychologically and logically explained and reviewed things – *but* the truth in that moment was that I did not love myself. Something shifted slightly, and as I walked back to the dormitory, it suddenly struck me as totally absurd that I had spent the whole afternoon wrestling with the truth that I did not love myself. What was the big deal? It seemed so ridiculous, so silly. In 'seeing' the truth as it is, something magical and wonderful happens. It is like it dissolves and becomes obsolete. Our resistance to a thing keeps it alive, gives it power, but our total acceptance with no need to change it brings about total transformation. There is so much that we think we do not want to be, and yet a beautiful freedom is offered in the complete acceptance of all things. This allows us to flow with life. No longer trapped like a caged bird you are free to spread your wings and fly. When you totally accept everything about yourself, there is nothing left to protect. All armour can be laid down and there is no pain or hurt triggered by something that anyone else could say to you.

That evening as I returned to the dormitory all desire to text Kevin had disappeared. The Dasas (the wonderful individuals guiding us) have asked for total silence until tomorrow morning. This feels easy. I'm pleased to do it. As I lay on my bed I realised that I had not thought of Kevin all afternoon. I am totally grateful to Edina for helping me see this part of myself. I feel complete peace and quiet and utterly content with life in its entirety. Right now there is nothing to protect, nothing to hide from myself or anyone else. Simply Peace and Quiet.

Another part of the process at The Oneness University is to help you get in touch with your creative capacity. Next, we were asked to think of our heart's desire and to visualise this during meditation. For some reason I have always had this vision of me speaking on stage to big groups of people. It doesn't really make sense to me because the idea of speaking in front of a group of people leaves me feeling cold and in a vice-like grip of fear. Anyway, I had nothing to lose so I decided to enter into the spirit of the activity. I visualise myself talking to big groups of people, starting with one or two in a small room and then expanding the space so that it eventually becomes many hundreds of people in an auditorium. I imagine it being an amazing experience, and while envisioning, a smile lights my whole face. I keep visualising and feeling until there is no fear, only a feeling of joy. When the meditation is over I am still curious as to how on earth I could speak to a room full of people and enjoy it! Funnily enough, the idea still makes my stomach churn.

The next day I was offered an amazing opportunity to practice. The process was now coming to an end and the course organiser asked if someone would like to come forward and thank the helpers on everyone's behalf. No one moved and I was feeling so much ecstatic joy, happiness and gratitude, that before I knew it I was on my feet and heading to the front of the room! There was no thought; I simply wanted to give them a hug to express my thanks. Unfortunately my joy came to an abrupt halt when a microphone suddenly confronted me. I froze, a huge knot of fear erupting in my solar plexus. Dread swept through me as I realised I had to say something. "Wow, I'm speechless," I mumbled. "They have all been so great." I couldn't get that microphone out of my hand fast enough. I felt dreadful and just wanted to crawl into a big hole to disappear forever. As I went back to my seat I thought, 'What an idiot you are.' I wished that I could have produced an elegant and brilliant speech. I'm sure you know the kind of thing, where I am graceful and confident in delivering a powerful speech that moves some to tears at the serious points, and conversely creates a ripple of laughter at just the right moment. My negative thoughts went into serious overdrive and started to bash me left, right and centre. I decided to put all that I had learned in the last few days into practice. I knew that the first step was to contain and allow the hideous uncomfortable feeling within – that's what I set out to do. I said a little prayer to the divine, 'Please help me stay with this discomfort,' and took a deep breath. It was time for a break. As I headed to the door a very eloquent, entertaining and lively Irish chap jokingly said to me, "Great speech, Wend!" I nearly went to say, "It was so shit," but instead chose to say nothing and just experience the increasing feeling of discomfort in my body. I just gently nodded, grimacing, and promptly left the hall.

After the break I returned to the hall, still feeling awful. I was breathing and attempting to allow the feeling, but to be honest, I was resisting because I wanted the feeling to disappear. I took my place and one of the senior Dasas was seated at the front to speak with us. He asked how everyone was and there followed a big ripple of, "We're great!" Then he asked if anyone was *not* okay. I was pondering whether to share because I certainly was *not* feeling great, but the thought of putting my hand in the air made me feel even worse. Yet another mental battle began to wage war within: 'Go on, put your hand up,' versus, 'No, don't!' Fear escalating at the idea of raising my hand, I silently asked for help to stay with the feeling. Eventually I thought, 'Okay, I'll do it,' just as another person's hand went into the air and beat me to it. Relief flooded through me and I felt momentarily better. 'Good,' I thought, 'I don't need to speak, I'll just stay with the feeling.' The knot eased for a moment but it was still there, and as I took a deep breath I suddenly realised the projection of the whole event. I saw that I didn't really experience speaking to the group because I had become gripped by fear instead. This meant I was not present to the experience, as my thoughts had become preoccupied with an escape route rather than what was happening in the moment. This had resulted in me being bombarded with worrying thoughts of messing it up and making a fool of myself, rather than thoughts of how wonderful the helpers were. As usual, I had been completely focused on myself rather than on others.

In that moment I decided to put my hand up and get the microphone a second time, only I was determined to actually experience the act. I did my best to focus on the woman who was speaking. When her exchange with the Dasa finished he told a beautiful story about how, when we fully experience life and all that it offers with these wonderful opportunities, we can break through limiting patterns that we hold - this was a perfect fit for me. When he finished speaking and looked around the room my hand shot up in the air. Well, this was it! The microphone was on its way. I had given no thought to what I was actually going to say, but as the microphone was handed to me I took a deep breath and said, "I would like all of your help to fully experience something that terrifies me. Grace offered me a wonderful challenge earlier and I ran away. What I would like to fully experience is this – speaking to a big group of people." I took a deep breath and began to roam about the room with my eyes. Everyone was staring at me and smiling. I bathed in the experience and allowed myself to experience that very moment – and do you know what – it actually felt very nice. "You are all really helping by staring at me, and actually it feels kind of nice. Thank you," I laughed. I glanced at the Dasa and nodded my gratitude. His smile was filled with warmth and there was a round of applause. I laughed some more and then the attention was moved on to the next person. I felt so happy. It was so liberating and I was buzzing.

As the session came to an end one of the UK ladies from the dormitory leaned over and said, "You sounded so relaxed and natural." As we were leaving the wonderful Irish chap said, "So, when are you taking up public speaking? That was brilliant!" Later that day a lady came and gave me a big hug and excitedly told me how much she enjoyed what I had said. My friends in the dormitory were supportive and the next day there were more compliments from people. It was amazing to receive such positive feedback from everyone. This opportunity really transformed all my preconceptions about speaking in front of a crowd. Apparently public speaking is the number one fear, but isn't it amazing how most of that fear is self-created and often not relevant to the actual experience itself. As the course came to an end I was continuing to feel fantastic and looking forward to seeing the girls and Kevin.

When we had first arrived in Chennai, given the long flight, Edina and I both opted to have a massage. I have received a handful of massages since my changed body, and initially it made me feel very uncomfortable. I felt ugly, disfigured and wretched. The massage on my arrival in Chennai was wonderful. I really enjoyed it and I felt more comfortable with my feet and body than ever before. The masseur massaged my legs, feet, head, neck and back. My torso remained covered under the towel. I was gradually becoming more comfortable with my body and I realise that the only important thing is how *I* feel and think about it. What anyone else thinks is irrelevant. The more comfortable I am the more comfortable everyone else is. It always makes me think of the programme X Factor when someone is auditioning or performing and they are so nervous that it's palpable. Often I have heard the judges say, "You were so nervous and that makes *us* feel nervous." It's not a good feeling and we can't wait for that person to leave the stage so we don't have to feel uncomfortable ourselves any longer.

Once we left the Oneness University I felt so completely peaceful and happy. We were lucky enough to spend some time in Chennai before an evening flight home. I decided to make the most of it, to do some shopping and enjoy a massage. Edina left for her massage first and I was sitting in the reception of the hotel having a drink, watching the world go by. I suddenly started thinking about 'The Divine Mother.' In our final gathering at the University we met in our countries. A number of people were saying about Amma, the divine mother, how beautiful she was and how they had felt her presence during the week. I had not noticed her at all, really. I felt some sort of connection with Bhagavhan but had hardly noticed Amma. Had we even had any teachings? I was not aware of any. Sitting in the hotel café I suddenly felt all soft and feminine. Gratitude flooded my body like a wave and a soft smile met my lips. It was nearly time for my massage so I visited the ladies. As I was sitting on the toilet I was blissfully aware of an incredible, sudden presence. It was so beautiful and radiant that I felt completely blessed. So, there I am sitting on the toilet feeling accompanied by the divine mother and being totally blissed out! Part of me was aware I was sitting on the toilet and thinking, 'I'm sitting on the toilet; surely there are more sacred places to receive a blessing?' And yet another part of me was moved to tears. I felt so much Love – so much Love for the world and I.

I headed upstairs for the massage, which was to bring yet more beautiful realisation. She massaged my legs before my arms. I had a moment of discomfort as she massaged my slightly hairy armpits (yes, again) but I just experienced it. I thought about the false belief of hairy armpits not being acceptable. If I were German I wouldn't care at all about them! This made me chuckle and the discomfort passed. The next part took me by surprise; she discreetly revealed my stomach, the sides of my torso and then massaged them. It felt so incredibly amazing, and far from feeling like I wanted to hide, I soaked up the touch. It felt so nourishing. During that massage I had no pain whatsoever in my body. This is the one and only time so far in my life that I have ever experienced this. I wondered if it was a 'mind in total peace.' When she had finished and I was dressed, I asked her if she would like to receive a Oneness Blessing. After some discussion in broken English she was smiling and replying, "Yes." She had not heard of the Oneness University or Oneness Blessing (just as I hadn't, previously). While she sat I placed my hands on her head and asked the divine to channel the blessing. After I had done so she sat for some time with her eyes closed. When she opened them, they were shining so brightly, she excitedly said, "I felt something!" and promptly jumped up and hugged me. Then she bowed down and touched my feet before jumping up and hugging me again. It was a beautiful moment.

Edina and I left the hotel and embarked on a shopping trip. Everything we wanted seemed to appear in front of us as if by magic. Because of that it made it a magical experience in itself, and I felt in a state of slightly altered awareness. I fell in love with India, all the sights, smells, colours and bustling life. The beautiful people. Part of me wanted to explore the country further and see more, but I was equally thrilled to be heading home to the girls and Kevin.

Shortly after returning home I received a call from the medical company who provided the piece of pigskin for my bowel operation. They were so pleased with the recovery I had made that they asked me if I was willing to come and talk to the staff at their plant in Leeds. This would mean talking to around forty people. I instantly accepted and laughed as I got off the phone at this bizarre 'out of the blue' invitation to speak in public! It struck me that there might be something in this visualisation lark, like invisible wheels put into motion.

A month later the day arrived. I prepared ten slides for my talk with images in chronological order showing the level of destruction at the first operation then the gradual recovery. I had thought I might be nervous but quickly realised there was nothing I could get wrong, this was simply me sharing my story. On the journey to Leeds I recited a lovely little mantra that I got from Wayne Dyer entitled 'How May I Serve?' I love this thought, it acts as a brilliant eliminator of fear. I find that when my thoughts are about me, something I desire or how I might get something wrong, there is fear. However, if I think of other people in ways that I can be helpful the fear disappears and is replaced by a wonderful feeling of joy. On arrival at the factory I was warmly greeted. After a cup of tea and a few hellos we set out on a guided tour, which started with a pig in a freezer. "Is it organic?" I joked as the chap lifted the lid of the freezer. As the tour unfolded a feeling of gratitude was growing within me. It was such a remarkably detailed process to create this medical product, I was blown away. I was consumed with gratitude for every single person (and pig) who was involved in creating this product, right from the person who had the idea, to the person who emptied the bins and cleaned the floor. I could see that everyone had a vital role to play and that all were absolutely necessary. It made me think about the value of people in teams and I could see this clearly in a hospital setting. I thought that you could have the best surgeon in the world, but if the room or instruments were not sanitised then his/her operations would not be successful.

When it was time for my talk I had hardly had a chance to think. I was in such a state of gratitude that I felt amazing. I began by looking around the room and smiling. I remembered to *allow* the experience, to be present to the moment rather than let any pre-emptive ideas run the show. The talk went smoothly and I can honestly say that at no point was I nervous. Everyone was really grateful to me for coming to speak and was moved by my experience. Yes, some people shed a tear but I also made them laugh too! I tell you, the feeling of thankfulness was out of this world. I was so very grateful to every single person sitting in that room; I bet they felt that. It seems to me that gratitude is not an emotion *per se*, rather it is a state of being which brings with it miraculous effects.

The other thing that had become wholly apparent was that I could view myself from a totally different perspective. I realised that I had been viewing myself from my own thoughts; all the past experiences and all the things over the years that I had come to believe made up whom I was. This was coupled with the events that were currently going on in my life as problems to be solved. I began to experience myself as energy rather than merely thoughts. It was fun to observe and play with. This had begun with the Oneness Retreat in Scotland. You see, when asked the question, "How do you feel right now?" you can't help but be pulled into the present moment... "Kicking and screaming," sometimes I might add. The more attached and identified you are with your life story/problems, the harder it is drag yourself into the present moment. The present moment offers you joy and spontaneous expression of your creativity, something that, unconsciously, we try to avoid for some strange reason. Perhaps we will never really understand why and it is not something to concern ourselves with. The important thing is how to get beyond the self-sabotage and blocks to Love. When asked the question of, "How do you feel right now?" you have to take a moment and consider how you feel *right now*. You will be astonished at just how difficult it is to answer this question when you are ensconced in some sort of drama. It's incredible. I began to see how attached I was to my stories, my problems, life's difficulties. As I started to explore the energy more I found I couldn't help be anything but present. It was also incredible because energy will always move, and you can literally change how you feel in a flash – BUT what usually happens is that we do all manner of things to keep it stuck. Again, who cares why? Note to self: Stop asking and trying to answer impossible questions and instead just do the things that move the energy – then you can be present and carry on and have fun... It is simple but wholly complicated by the intellect. When I am completely present there is always peace and joy. Everything else just melts away and it is like looking at the world through a different set of eyes. I used to get pulled out of it by thinking I HAD TO DO something, but what I have come to realise is that DOING spontaneously arises from BEING. Any pressure of the necessity or need to do is usually some sort of avoidance on my part. When the state is BEING, the DOING takes care of itself. It's a bit like watching yourself moving around in the world, it's fun! For me it was like a brand new experience of the world and myself in it; a whole new way of BEING was beginning to emerge.

Chapter 9
Wendy's World is Falling Down!

After returning from India I continued with my degree and my relationship with Kevin flourished. I was in a good space and very happy. At the end of 2009 I attended a business seminar in London. I was totally inspired to begin a business to share what I had discovered to help others. To create this I put my degree on hold and embarked on launching a coaching business, working with a mentor. I wanted to share with others this gorgeous altered awareness that had been revealed to me, and how to move through and flow with emotions. I wanted to share peace and happiness, so that we could finally all be free of the past and instead create a new future with more Love, peace and abundance. I published my first book *Process and Prosper: Why it's essential to cry, get angry and stamp your feet and how it can save your life*, invested heavily with a mentor, and boldly stepped forward to take the world by storm. I was determined to master this 'create your own reality'/law of attraction thing' to manifest what I wanted and help others to do the same. Speaking gigs had arisen out of nowhere. Kevin had also shown up after I'd completed the manifesting activity whilst at the retreat in Scotland. 'Why not anything else?' I wondered. I immersed myself in *Think and Grow Rich* by Napoleon Hill and *The Science of Getting Rich* by Wallace Wattles, as well as learning about business, marketing, sales and all the technology to create a website. Then there was social media, not to mention the time working with clients, attending events and networking. It was full-on!

I found out that I loved video as a medium and so I had started using this as a tool to share. I was working at the kitchen table one day in April 2010 when my phone beeped. It was from Ro. All our communication over the last couple of years had only been about practical arrangements with Martha, so I was surprised at what it said.

'What are you working on creating at the moment?'

I can't remember what I replied but I asked after him. He sent a cryptic reply about feeling like he was under glass. I had my suspicions that he was not totally happy in his relationship and thought he meant that.

'Why? What's up?' I sent.

I was shocked at the reply.

'You are the unscratchable itch.'

Shit! What to say to that? I had hurt him so many times in the past I couldn't bear to do it again. As much as I knew that I had never stopped loving him I did not want to run the risk of hurting him again. I was aware of my track record and it wasn't good! Plus I was with Kevin, and although it wasn't a bed of roses, I had made a commitment and was in it for the long haul. I had decided that I was too quick to throw in the towel in the past and that it was me I needed to work on and that was what I was doing.

After a moment of thought I sent, 'I think we tried really hard and it doesn't work. Now I just love you and know that that's okay.'

'Maybe. We'll see,' came the reply.

I still missed Ro when I thought about him. We seemed to have this incredible bond, something that I could not understand, and I never doubted that I still loved him very much. Over our years apart I had discovered that it was when I had denied my love for him that I hurt. When I accepted my love for him it always put a smile on my face, but I did not need him or have the need to possess him, and I certainly didn't want to create more pain in break-ups. I had done enough of that in the past. This time I was doing my best to be as mature and as loving as I possibly could.

I let all thoughts of Ro go and carried on with the business and my relationship with Kevin, together with our attempts to harmoniously combine our family units. It strikes me that extended families are wonderful opportunities to learn to love. Presenting opportunities to love fully with all your heart, even though it is not your flesh and blood – by allowing the chance to practice acceptance of others' ways of doing things, even though they may be different from your own, is extremely liberating.

In the summer of 2010 Kevin and I moved into separate homes. Our attempts to combine our families, sadly had proved too much of a challenge for us. We decided that it was in everyone's best interests to have some space. I soon moved to a lovely place with Amy and Martha and we partook in weekend gatherings. It wasn't great but we muddled on. I was under increasing pressure with the business. I'd played a big game, invested heavily with borrowed money and hadn't managed to actually make much money. I felt under intense pressure all the time. The tension in my neck was unbearable. My mentor was coaching me to charge higher prices but I felt uncomfortable about it. I was in a state of paralysis. One night I decided that I had had enough. I'd made a huge mistake and would just have to take the consequences and say I couldn't do it! I decided that I would stay quiet for two days to rest in silence before I took any action.

On the second day I was sitting in the garden when I suddenly 'experienced' that the Universe *was* abundant. It was one of those moments of revelation where an intellectual idea about a Spiritual Principle expands in the mind and meets with the essence of life itself – very much like the tree incident on the Tai Chi retreat. I knew, without a shadow of doubt, that my thoughts were creating my reality. Therefore, just because I had, didn't mean that another went without. I immediately created a high-level coaching program and within two weeks I had filled nine places. I felt like I'd cracked it and with the money coming in – it was brilliant. I began working with the clients, sharing law of attraction principles and delving into the blocks to allowing ourselves to receive. I was in a completely altered state and very much 'in flow.' I found new business prospects and clients very easy to find because they just showed up.

I ran events, worked with clients and it was always really amazing. Somehow I seemed to know things about people on a very deep level; I could 'feel' them and the right thing to say just appeared in my mind. I didn't trust this source of information at first, but just like the writing and the poems, a sentence would appear in my mind. It would repeat itself until I spoke it out loud. Each time I did I would discover that it was the perfect information to help the person before me, and gradually I began to trust it more and more.

Towards the end of the program however, I started to feel out of sorts. I had wanted to take them to the altered state that I had achieved to see them bust through their limitations, especially the financial ones in the way that I had. It hadn't happened and I felt terrible. It was time to find another group of people to run the program again. I just felt completely paralysed and contracted. The idea of marketing and sales actually filled me with dread. I'd lost that glorious altered state, along with my mojo.

I was confused and was really pondering who was in control. Was I? Or was there something greater? Having had the experiences of the writing, the NDE, the Tai Chi Tree expansion and so on, I had this sense that there was something more, but I just couldn't quite grasp it. I was curious as to whether I was creating/manifesting with my own conscious thoughts or whether something greater was moving through me. You see, on several occasions I had an absolute 'knowing' that something was going to happen and then it did. I would 'see' myself (like a vision) doing something and then it would come to pass. This somehow felt different than focusing my intellectual thinking on manifesting something, as it was always accompanied by an absolute peaceful knowing. I had the sense of something inwardly nudging me towards something more than I could currently comprehend.

In my desperation I leafed through a copy of a book called *The Way of Mastery* one day at my friend's house when the following prayer jumped out at me. I wrote it down and began to recite it, morning and night:

'Source, Creator, God, Goddess, All That Is, Abba
I am ready to be what you created me to be.
I choose to remember that I am effect and not cause.
Thy will be done, knowing that your will is my full happiness.
Reveal then, that path through which that happiness can be

known.
For my way has never worked, but your way always does.'

One night in February 2011 I woke in the early hours. It was two am. Oddly, I felt like I'd been woken up by something. This was a familiar feeling, one that was usually followed by a torrent of writing. This time however, because I had been making the videos I decided to switch on the video and just started to natter. This process went on for ten days. Every night I got woken up and every night I put the video on and nattered away until I ran out of things to say, or when sleep overtook me. On occasion I felt so exhausted I would think, 'Oh no, not again... I just want to sleep.' Then this thought would arise... 'This is about the evolution of humankind. Can you get out of bed for that?' It certainly seemed something worth getting out of bed for, worth being tired for, so I would drag myself out of bed and turn on the video.

It began with vast stories of regret; so much about Ro and how wonderful it had been, about how I'd ruined it, etc. Gradually as the nights wore on, it was as if I became so tired that all my barriers fell down. On the one hand I was functioning on a couple of hours' sleep a night, but was as high as a kite. On the other hand I felt completely fragile and delicate. I was trying to work on the business during the day but I couldn't concentrate. All I wanted to do was keep the fire burning in the living room. Ironically, it was a wood burner right in the centre of the room. I kept finding myself saying, "One becomes two, two becomes four, four becomes eight," and so it continues. It appeared to me that all of life was created by the one source separating itself again and again, over and over.

The first few days were the stories of regret; all the things I'd ever done wrong or messed up and all the people I'd hurt. I could see so much fuel for the guilt and shame that held me hostage to my past and stopped me from living in the present. As these layers and stories gradually dissolved and loosened their grip, my awareness began to expand. I began to experience the connection between all things and the connection between all beings. The world suddenly seemed like an amazing place full of endless creation; all my senses were heightened. One evening I went for dinner with friends at a local pub and the food was 'out of this world' tasty!

The weather had been really cold and so I had brought my rabbits inside in their hutch. As I set the video up one afternoon a clear thought arose, 'Put the rabbits outside.' I couldn't be bothered to move the hutch and simply continued to set up my video. I then knelt down and pressed record. All of a sudden the rabbits started making a complete racket, scrabbling and running around. Then this thought, 'We told you to put the rabbits out.' I froze and listened intently. I can't say I hear a voice because there is no sound, but it is definitely more like a sentence or statement arising in my mind. It was different to my usual analytical thought, and for ease of communicating with you; I'll call it 'the wisdom' because it's always wise, expansive, loving and kind. It was very much like the wisdom that communicated with me telepathically when I had my near death experience. Maybe it's even the same.

'We've been speaking to you for a long time now,' said the wisdom. 'You thought you were very clever,' it continued, with humour, loving and kindness. This was in such a way that, far from feeling silly or criticised it just made me laugh because, yes, I had thought that.

It told me about the divine union of man and woman. That woman was the power source for life and creation and that man was the valiant knight who went forth into the world to create things in form. He was strong and courageous in the world and his absolute joy was to make, build and construct material things in the world. He would go out being energised and enthused by her Love before gradually becoming depleted. At this point he would return to her Love to be re-energised. She would be nourished by his Love, respect and adoration of her – her absolute joy is to nourish, replenish and care. Her supply is bountiful, provided by the heavens, for it comes from the endless supply of Unconditional Love, which is the source of all life itself. Together they are the glorious union of opposites, which combine into creation. Either one cannot exist in isolation but rather it is their union from which life, as we know it, bursts forth.

I felt like, as woman, that was what I wanted. I wanted to fully Love a man and pour my Love into him, but given willingly and not taken. It was my greatest joy to do this with the knowledge that my power supply was infinite. It felt like the world was out of balance, that men and women were confused as to who they were. This left us feeling out of sorts which then resulted in the chaos we were experiencing in the world.

We need change. We need a new way of Being and sharing in the world. We need the Mother Love to return to being something that is valued and treasured instead of crushed and despised. She is mighty and powerful but not something to be feared as is reflected in our current paradigm. She is the bringer of peace, sharing and equity. In this moment I understood what the tarot card lady had seen, the dark area in my abdomen that she had said was Mother issues – it was related to the depths of the feminine itself. This was about the Divine Mother and my relationship with her. This was about femininity.

As much as I love and adore the wisdom in always feeling utterly magical in its presence, for some strange reason I repeatedly run away in the other direction. I also experienced more of the opposite with the clutches of fear beckoning me, wrapped up in stories of paranoia. One night the video camera card was full and I realised I had left my laptop downstairs. As I went into the hallway and flicked on the light switch the bulb blew and tripped out the lights. I felt totally petrified, immediately ducking back in my room, slamming the door. I leant my back against it, breathing hard. Panic was racing in me, contracting my body and my thoughts were filled with negativity. I had the idea that people were out to get me. That someone was in my home and would be coming up the stairs at any moment.

As I leaned on the door my mind was racing, frantically attempting to decide what to do. It was pitch black and I couldn't see a thing, but suddenly I remembered that my phone was on the dressing table. I grabbed it and dialled Kevin's number. Thankfully he answered. I started to garble what had happened and how scared I was. He was great. He listened, talked me off the mental insanity track I was on (by gently laughing at my thoughts) and even offered to come over. After a few moments I felt much calmer. He had his kids at home and I didn't want him to disturb them and so I said I was fine. I decided that I would simply get into bed and do my best to go to sleep. No videoing for me tonight.

The fear and panic did subside and in the morning I woke feeling relieved and having a chuckle at myself. Blimey! I could see why people started to tell conspiracy theory stories. It felt like a layer of denial, a layer of separation. Another barrier to the Love that is all there is. It was so enticing, so gripping that I could see why people put tin foil on their heads. It seems to me that this is simply also another layer of block, one that is easy to get gripped by.

The next day was quite challenging as I was wondering about my sanity. I felt so weak and fragile, not like a good mum at all. I didn't even want to go out of the house. Amy snapped at me about something, it was only minor, but it upset me so much that I burst into tears! I went round the corner of the living room to the kitchen and slumped down on the floor with my head in my hands. Next moment Martha trotted round with a box of colouring pens, pencils and paper.

"Here you are, Mummy," she said calmly. "Draw pictures of Love. It will make you feel better."

I looked up at her slightly confused. "Pictures of Love?" I asked quizzically.

"Yes," she replied, matter-of-factly. "Draw pictures of hearts and flowers. Pictures of Love. It will make you feel better."

"Oh, okay," I agreed and took the book she handed me.

She sat down beside me with her own book, handed me a piece of paper, took one herself and started to draw. I followed suit and picked up a pen and drew a heart. Before I knew it I was writing about Love, drawing a rainbow with hearts and flowers all over my piece of paper. It worked and I did feel better. There is a quality of insight and understanding that emanates from Martha that I do not quite understand. She has the ability to make me feel so much better and, right now if it wasn't for her, I would be worried about my mental health.

That night I reached a pinnacle point; there was a moment where I KNEW that there was only me. That *I* was projecting and creating the whole world that I saw. For a brief moment I rested in Love's absolute silence before fear began to speak. It gave me images akin to the likes of *I am Legend*, that movie with Will Smith; images of me wandering alone in the barren and desolate streets of Exeter. With all people having disappeared, my children disappearing before fear opened its arms with me running full pelt into them. Give me the separation, give me what I think I know; don't give me infinity and 'nothingness' because I sure as hell don't want the peace of endless serenity.

Fears journey was slow at first, I felt fragile and vulnerable and attacked at every angle. All I wanted to do was keep the fire burning. The outside world seemed like a harsh and cruel place that I did not want to be in. I wanted to hide and never come out. Instead I had a business to run and clients to find. I simply couldn't function as everything filled me with dread. I couldn't sleep properly, my whole body was contracted and tense and I felt filled with fear and worry. About the only thing I could do was smoke. Great tactic to attempt to push the feelings down but I couldn't cope; I was literally engulfed in fear and couldn't function and I fell flat on my face! I pulled the plug on my business, went bankrupt and dived into a deep, dark pit full of guilt and shame.

Where had the amazing altered reality gone? Was I going mad? Losing my mind?

Unfortunately, things went from bad to worse. My relationship with Kevin broke down and my dad died all within a few weeks. It seemed like everything was being stripped away at once. It felt like everything was gone and I was being punished in some way. I was in a whirlwind of fear and despair. This catapulted me into my loneliness, and the deep despair and fear that accompanied it.

I was desperate to do something, anything, and start earning some money. The first thing I could find was a cleaning job, which I took. It was for a building plant hire company just down the road, cleaning for an hour at the end of each day. Because it was so close I cycled to it. There were a couple of nice chaps who managed the place and worked in the office. Each evening they would be leaving as I arrived and we always exchanged pleasantries. A couple of weeks in as I arrived on my bike, one of the guys smiled and said, "What will you do in the winter?" He was referring to me on my bike. My immediate thought was, 'I won't be here in the winter,' but I just smiled and replied, "Not sure." The next day it was absolutely hammering down with rain so I decided to take the car. The bankruptcy was under way and I knew the car would be repossessed at some point as it had outstanding finance. The car I had was quite a nice one, a Lexus IS 220d, and the sort of thing you would expect to see an executive driving. I will never forget the look on the manager's face as I pulled up in the Lexus and got out. He was just pulling away in his car and did a complete double take, before looking really confused and then nodding to me as he drove away. I couldn't help but chuckle, and as I went about cleaning the toilets and office floor it struck me that this was an amazing lesson in humility. Which part of me thought I was too good to clean the toilets? Why did I think I was superior or better than anyone else? I could see how my ego had really got caught up in the manifesting and how I had thought I was powerful, and yet there was so much that I didn't know.

The next evening when I arrived on my bike the manager was still in the office. As I came in and said, "Hi," he smiled at me and exclaimed with a quizzical smile, "So, what is it that you do?" I smiled, "Ahhh," I said. "I'm in transition. I did start my own business but it didn't work out the way I had hoped."

"I thought you were a little different," he said.

The following months were tough. I felt dreadful most of the time, with knots of twisted fear and anxiety within.. I woke one night in total discomfort. The emotional pain was so great that I didn't know what to do with myself. I had never felt this way before. I tried to just 'be' and breathe deeply. I tried to invite the loving presence, but the sense of anxiety and self-hatred was so intense that I needed to do something, anything. I couldn't stand it. My hand balled into a fist and I punched my thigh. It hurt a bit but strangely brought some modicum of relief. I punched my thigh again, harder this time. It gave me slight relief but not enough. I hated myself so much in that moment! I then proceeded to punch myself in the face. First one side, then the other. It hurt! It also broke the vice-like grip of self-loathing that had cloaked itself around me and held me captivate in its destructive arms. Hot tears coursed down my cheeks. Finally I could breathe as the sobs wracked throughout my body. Eventually I drifted off to sleep. In the morning I looked in the mirror at the two slightly black eyes staring back at me. There was only one thought in my mind... 'I NEED HELP!'

I rang Ruth and confessed what I had done to myself. One of the best things you can do with anything shameful or guilt-ridden is share it with someone who will support you. Ruth was great as always and I made a decision right then to get some help. I didn't know where to go because I didn't want to go down the counselling route. Having had these spiritual experiences I wanted and needed someone who could meet me in that place. I had no idea who that was, and so instead just decided that I was open to help.

The next week I went to the Oneness Blessing group. A couple of them were talking about how they had been to stay with a lady called Asha for four days of healing. I knew of Asha as her name had been in our circle for a few months. She did energy healing; something inside me knew this was the right way to go. I duly arranged a four-day stay with her in Scotland for the next month.

Chapter 10
Lost and Found

'The truth shall set you free but first it'll piss you off' – Gloria Steinem

November 2011

Martha and Amy have gone to stay with Mum and I'm up in Scotland with Asha. It's been amazing so far. The prevalence of the guilt and shame, such powerfully strong emotions, have been making me think about an idea that I picture of how one would arrive at the pearly gates after death. Well, maybe not the pearly gates but some sort of someone or council of someones who would be with me as I reflect on my life looking at the good things, but more importantly, the bad things that I have done. In this meeting I would share the bird's-eye view and see it in perspective. There would be a chance to repent and then on I'd happily skip, totally free of the burdens of a life on earth. It's been making me think about this because it feels like it's happening now – but I am not dead, I am alive. The first two days have been incredible, this woman truly is remarkable. I also understand that I am remarkable and that it is our own ability to embrace what's offered that allows for our growth, release and liberation.

It's been very releasing working with Asha as I have seen many things in my own mind and myself. I have been reminded how, when I am completely present to the moment, glorious spontaneous joy arises. I'd forgotten that; about how there is only joy in this state and how I smile for no reason and feel peaceful and at rest. I have seen how often I am not present to the moment but instead get caught up in thought – caught up in regrets, self-punishment and analysis – completely missing what is happening in the moment right now. I can see how these thoughts and ideas grab my attention and, where they are combined with emotion, they send me off like a racehorse from the stalls along the track of thought, totally consumed by it and lost in its believability. It's really quite incredible and the negativity is so powerful that it's like pollution.

Last night was funny. I went to help make the dinner and I can honestly say that my intention was to go and help to cook and have a nice chat. However, it wasn't long before I found myself – yet again – talking about Ro with my regrets and woes surrounding it. All of a sudden I heard myself and looked over at Asha.

"Am I doing it again?" I asked.

"Yes, Sweetie," she replied. "It's like you are farting into the lovely fresh air!" She began to chuckle.

I also burst out laughing because I could see exactly what she meant. She was quite happy, joyful and peaceful in the moment in her kitchen cooking away, when I come in and start talking about my woes. Of course, they're all wrapped up in sadness, regret and what we might refer to as the heavier emotions. I could really see how addicted to the whole thing I was and that it was not serving me very well. All it was doing was making me feel pretty shit. In that moment it was obvious. It seemed extremely funny. I literally chose *not* to talk or think about it and discuss something else instead. The subject kept popping into my head but each time it did I just said, 'thanks' and didn't attach to it. We had a very pleasant evening, full of laughter and lightness.

Day 3

Sometimes the bitterest pills, once swallowed, create the most amazing transformations. More and more over the years I have come to realise that it's not the details of a story that are important, it's allowing oneself to really feel the emotions without resistance and judgement which will create that lasting transformation. In fact, what I have increasingly seen is that the more I am attached to the story the more stuck I become. I remain in an endless trap from which I can never escape as the same stories arise again and again. These stories are just wrapped in slightly different packaging or even in exactly the same packaging. If you think about it, we all tell the same stories but somehow we believe they are unique to us and we take them very personally. What I was experiencing all the more was when I allowed the emotions about something to happen, I would find peace and a sense of freedom that I'd never had before. I began to see these repeating patterns all over the place.

I feel like I came to Asha with my 'Wendy Map' of the world and she pointed out that it was faulty. I looked at it and it wasn't easy because I had invested many years in that map and I found that, unconsciously, I was protecting it. I saw that she was right. Now suddenly I am without a map. I will share the profound insight that she gifted to me in the hope that it may liberate you as well.

What Asha said was this: "You are leading with your wounds." Now, as you know I have had a pretty big experience. She wasn't talking about this; she was talking about emotional wounds. She was talking about being in an intimate relationship and bringing in my problems and issues. When she first said it I wanted to protest, I wanted to defend my right to share it in that way. Surely that is what an intimate relationship is about, the deep sharing of each other? However, this is another thing that years of emotional recovery have taught me. If I immediately wish to defend or justify something or in other words, something ruffles my feathers, then somewhere I have a problem. Very commonly how we go about it, because it's what we've been taught, is we discuss it. Another thing that I have learned is that this can keep me going round in circles for years. This is because the real answers are not in my intellect; they are not in justification *or* rationalisation and no one else has them. The best answers and insights are found in the silence of my being. I'll explain… when Asha said, "You're leading with your wounds," and I felt I immediately wished to defend my position to her verbally, instead what I did was the exact opposite. I shut up and turned my attention to myself. I resisted the urge to speak or defend, and in doing so, this instantly revealed an immense anger. I was sitting on the floor, so I wrapped my arms around my legs and buried my head in my knees.

The anger welled up inside and I was so pissed off with her. Thoughts began to invade my mind such as, 'How dare she say that? She's got no idea what I have been through! Why shouldn't I talk about those things? What does *she* know anyway?' I took a deep breath and I promised myself to 'own' that this was *my* problem and that I was projecting it out onto *her*. I knew I had to take responsibility and bring it back to me. Grudgingly, I took a deep breath. The feeling of anger was strong, like a raging bull. I forced myself to take another deep breath and, whilst taking a mental step back, focused all my attention on the physical feeling in my body. The onslaught of invading and distracting thoughts continued to infest my mind, but their grip was loosened by the choice to *own* my problem. I've since found this works every time a challenge is presented to me; the moment that I remember to see it as a gift is the moment that the whole thing begins to unravel. Keeping my awareness on my breath, as I watched the feeling of anger it began to dissipate. In its place came a deep sadness. Again, I breathed. The tirade of thoughts silenced themselves as the overwhelming sadness made itself known like a deep and never-ending well. The tears began to silently fall from my eyes as I let myself fall, deeper and deeper, tumbling down and down. Suddenly there was nothing and I could not remember what I was doing. I don't know how long this took; it took as long as it needed to. Very slowly I raised my head from my knees, looked her square in the eyes and humbly asked, "Please would you tell me that again?" Softly Asha replied, "Yes. You are leading with your wounds."

Immediate anger sprung up yet again so I reburied my head in my knees and resumed my breathing. Again, the bottomless well of sadness opened before me and I dived right in. I repeated the words to myself as I fell deeper and deeper. The protesting part of me was speechless; it had lost its grip. Its powerful influence quelled. Like a slithering snake it retreated from whence it came. All that was left was the silence of the deep well, echoing its resounding reminder about leading with wounds. As this concept penetrated my awareness the wisdom suddenly came to meet it. 'Yes,' it said. 'It's what you have all been conditioned to do. Pain creates pain. You do not mean to, but you are in pain, and so unwittingly you create pain in others.' In an instant it was crystal clear. We are all wounded and we go around wounding others because pain creates pain. It doesn't mean to because it's unconscious and not malicious or anything, it's just what it does. I see how, when I am in emotional pain I use the outside world to try and alleviate it. I share my woes and express my negative feelings. I blame others, I condemn myself... all attempts to make myself feel better, BUT what I see is these attempts are flawed and will never work to alleviate the deep internal pain that I feel. It's flawed because all this crazy cycle does is serve to maintain and perpetuate itself by causing further pain and wounding ourselves further. Yet this is deeply unconscious.

I raised my head again and asked her, "Should I not talk about my problems then? But I'm talking to you?"

"Sweetie!" she replied, firmly. "I'm a therapist. We are in a healing relationship."

Joy surged through my body like a flooding river. A smile spread magically across my lips and I burst out laughing. I could now see it so clearly. I had indeed been leading with my wounds. They were all I had and I had been so attached to them. What was I without my worries and woes? What would I talk about? What would I share? I could see the immense amount of investment in my persona, in who I thought I was and even 'what' I thought I was. Of course, it was obvious. You talk to the right person for the job. I didn't need to burden my intimate partner with my issues, as it was not their job to support me.

Day 4

This morning while I was receiving a lovely treatment from Asha on her couch that same deep sense of shame and guilt arose. I cannot recognise it as a particular issue, rather it feels sort of all-encompassing. The emotional pain inside is intense and I do not know what to do next. All of a sudden Martha is in my awareness.

"You have to forgive yourself, Mummy," she says.

"But I don't know how," I reply desperately.

"See yourself how I see you. See yourself with my eyes," she says.

Suddenly I am overwhelmed by the most amazing Love. It totally wraps me and I dissolve into tears; I am simultaneously bathed and cleansed. Everything melts and I know that I could have done the most heinous atrocities and I would still be loved. The thought is that I could have killed every single person on the planet and I would still be loved. There is no crime too great that in this Love will not be forgiven. The tears fall as I repeat over and over, "I'm so sorry." I mean it with all of my heart and soul for any wrong doings that I have ever done. A Love so pure and powerful fills my whole being; the tears subside and rapturous joy floods through me. Absolute peace fills my awareness and encompasses me completely.

Day 5

I can't wait to see the girls, I've missed them. As I arrive at Mum's Martha comes running up to me. "Are you okay?" she asks me with a strange tone in her voice.

"Yeeesss!" I reply, looking at her slightly suspiciously and thinking, 'What do you know?'

"I came to you, Mummy," she says. "I came to you because you needed me."

"I know you did, sweetheart," I say. "Thank you." I wrap my arms around her and we share a really big cuddle.

We returned home that night and it was back to school the next morning. On the way to pick her up I suddenly thought, 'I wonder if she loves everyone like that.'

So I asked her. "Hey Marfs, do you love everyone like that or just me?"

The reply astounded me. "Oh Mummy, I love everyone like that. I go round and knock on their hearts. Some people's hearts are open but some are closed."

A tear trickled down my cheek. "Wow, that's really beautiful."

"We need more love, Mummy," she concluded.

And she's right. We do need more love. We need more tolerance, more acceptance and greater understanding. We need to embrace our differences and heal our old hurts so that we can create peace and harmony in our world. I really do believe that we can experience heaven on earth. However, we will not get there by making changes to the outside world but instead by making shifts in our inner world, in our minds, which will in turn alter our perception. Peace will arise by allowing ourselves to return to the Love that is quietly and patiently waiting for us, and then allowing that to be expressed through us and shared with the world.

Chapter 11
Learning to Love

25th December 2011

Well, we've made it to Christmas. After severely worrying about the lack of money and how I was going to cope with Christmas, all is well. For the first time ever I was very sensible with money and cut right back. The kids have been amazing about it. Amy is spending the day at her dad's with Katy. Martha is with me and Mum is on her way down. We're going to my friend Sue's for Christmas dinner and I'm really looking forward to it. Martha and I have had a lovely morning. I got her lots of 'make and do' things. Ro's mum Trish has just texted to say 'Happy Christmas.' She's at her house in France. I go and shower and am just getting dressed when my phone beeps again. I do love Christmas time and all the warm greetings. It's Ro. He is due to be having Martha tomorrow and I expect it to be a text for her saying 'Happy Christmas.'

The text reads, 'Happy Christmas. Will have to reschedule Martha's visit due to events at home.'

Having recently fully embraced that him and Ruby are together forever I wonder whether they are both okay. I hope no one is ill or hurt.

I texted back, 'Happy Christmas. Are you okay?'

The reply… 'Yep. At Mum's. My fault.'

I sit on the bed in shock. Crikey. They have split up. I can't prevent the joy that surges through my system and the smile that spreads over my face. I immediately think he is in France, having just been in contact with his mum, but quickly realise that he must be down the road at her other house.

I texted back. 'Why don't you pop over and surprise Martha? It would make her day.'

He replies, 'That would be nice. I'll be over in about half an hour.'

I deliberately let Martha get the door saying that it must be Nanny. Her face is a picture. It's a bit surreal to have him at our house, in our lounge playing games and chatting. I love it though. I adore being around him and my heart beats in overdrive. He stays for an hour or so. I don't pry; just make sure he is okay. I offer for him to stay with us if he needs to, as I know his mum's house is pretty full. I can hardly contain my excitement. I keep trying to be rational in my head. I know nothing of the situation, they may well get back together, but I just can't contain the buzzing feelings at the thought of him returning to me. Thank you Father Christmas, it's the best gift ever!

27th December

Ro came today to see Martha – and I hoped me too.

There came a quiet moment where Martha went upstairs to do something and I asked him what happened. He explained that basically the relationship was not enough but that there was someone else who was enough. At this line my heart skipped a beat.

"And who is it that is enough?" I enquired gently while my insides were doing cartwheels at the thought of our reunion.

He replied, "Someone at work."

Fuck! My gut wrenched and I thought I might throw up. I tried to remain cool but just wanted to run away and burst into tears. I really thought he was going to say, "It's you." Thankfully, Martha came trotting back into the room right at that moment and so I could make a hasty exit under the ruse of making a cup of tea. In the sanctuary of the kitchen I leaned over the sink and took a deep breath followed by another, then another. 'Pull yourself together,' I said to myself. Talk about gutted! I felt like someone had ripped my heart out... again!

Shortly afterwards he came in the kitchen. "Are you okay?" he tentatively asked.

I decided to be honest. "No, but I will be. I thought you were coming back for me."

"Oh," he said. "I thought you suddenly changed."

"Yeah, it was a bit of a shock."

I asked a couple more questions but didn't really want to know anything much about the new lady yet. The rest of the afternoon was pleasant. He gingerly asked if it was still okay to take me up on my offer and stay. I said yes because it's nice for Martha to see him and I was enjoying seeing him as well. We had chatted a bit more over the day and it had been oddly therapeutic, with the chance to make some apologies and understand what happened between us a little more. We never really talked properly before. I had blamed myself so much over the years for being unfaithful and being caught up in myself. It was a blessing to be having this conversation some five years on when time had made it all less painful and eyes had been opened to see more clearly. I was curious as to why he hadn't helped me more if he was already aware of the peace. This was something that I had come to realise over the years; all my nagging about reading books about Presence when he didn't need to read them because he was already present. It made me chuckle the day I really saw that. He said that he didn't really know but that he could see he had left me emotionally and for that he was sorry. It was beautiful to share with such honesty, forgiveness and Love. Nothing really left to even be sorry for.

As I said, I adored having him around and thoroughly revelled in his energy. There is something about him and it feels so good to me. At one point we were in the kitchen/diner, he was with Martha in the dining area and I was cooking in the kitchen. My phone beeped with a text message and I was surprised when I saw it was from Ro.

It said, 'Perfect moment.'

I glanced over at him and smiled. It was indeed a perfect moment but that was all it was, a moment, because very soon he would leave to go and be with his new lady.

His behaviour was confusing because I was watching him checking for texts and messages from the new woman before becoming very flirty with me. We spent New Year's Eve together with Martha, playing lots of music and dancing. It was really good fun, it was where I wanted to be. At the stroke of midnight he gave me a kiss. I was so stunned that I totally missed that moment and had pulled back before I had even had a chance to think. Afterwards I wished I hadn't. His kisses were always so amazing, but there it was. The reality was that he was not with me; he was sadly off somewhere else.

New Year's Day was pleasant. In the evening I had arranged to visit a friend. As I was leaving he said, "When you get back we can watch a film, if you like."

I knew I had to draw a line and so I looked him in the eye and said…

"What are you doing? I'm watching you texting and e-mailing your new lady and then flirting with me. So are you going over there or are you coming here?"

He took a breath. "Sorry," he replied. "I can't seem to help myself with you but I am going over there."

"Okay, good," I said. "In that case I'm going out and I'm not coming back until tomorrow. Please stop flirting with me because it's really unkind. You know how I feel about you."

Despite this I still smiled at him and was surprised that I actually felt okay. I guess all those years of finding my way to a place of acceptance of him being with someone else still remained and therefore nothing was really any different. I wished him and Martha a fun evening together, grabbed an overnight bag and left the house.

Was I imagining it? That powerful energy between us again. Was I being ridiculous? That evening I did my best to forget about Ro completely and simply enjoy myself. I did a pretty good job. As I was driving home the next day I was pondering the connection and thought I would do a little test when I got home. I asked Ro if he would stand right in front of me. No funny business, no compromise, just a moment to look at each other and connect. I wanted to check that I wasn't imagining it all. He lasted all of about three seconds before he said…

"I can't do this," and moved away.

'Good,' I thought. 'I'm not going mad and making it up.'

I also knew in that moment that I needed to let him go and not to try and hold on in any way. Send him on his way with love. I actually felt empowered. Empowered by making a good wholesome decision, one that respected us all. Finally I understood Love, real Love. Real Love does not judge, criticise or condemn. It is forever present and all-encompassing. It gently offers a never-ending flow of forgiveness, which results in no past to hold a grudge about and no future thoughts to create fear. I began to experience a very different state compared to the one who had been wanting, punishing and seeking for so long. This new state was peaceful, aware and happy whatever was happening. All I wanted was for him to be happy, whatever that meant and whoever that was with. I did not need him to be with me; I did not need to possess him in any way and also my happiness was not dependent on him being with me. I also finally understood acceptance. Acceptance brings complete and total peace. I had no control over the external circumstances and I had no argument with them either. I felt immense peace and a sense that all was perfect just as it was. Over that period I chose to let go. I chose to stop arguing with God/Life and simply let it be as it was. With a new year on the horizon I decided it was time for a fresh start.

This wisdom has gifted me with many poems over the years, always about Love, connection and Oneness. I finally really understood this one:

Real Love

Real Love is not the initial passion,
The spark or the flurry
That puts your heart in a hurry.

Real Love is not the animal attraction,
The giddy obsession
Or need for possession.

Real Love is deeper than this
it is all there really is.

Real Love is what we all are,
No judgement or shame
No guilt or blame.

Real Love sees the perfection in all,
It's a heart wide open
Not just a token.

Real Love is not fragile or can ever be broken,
It's not dashing or charming
Secret or alarming.

Real Love is not smitten or clouded vision,
It's not a projection
Or the object of your affection.

Real Love takes you beyond the divide,
It opens eyes wide
Leaving nowhere to hide.

Real Love is all there is and ever will be,
The truth in plain sight
Life's pure delight.

Real Love is what you are
A timeless state from afar.

Chapter 12
Finding Faith

January 2012

I had an interview for a job at the Salvation Army. I'd been looking for something at twenty hours a week, to ease myself back out into the world. My conscious thinking was that I was looking for a coach or consultant who had their own business and had grown to the point of needing support so they could expand. Someone to come and organise all the behind the scenes activities for the business and the day-to-day running, so they could focus on their clients. Yet, I'd been inspired to get the paper one day. There was an advert for a financial administration assistant at the local Salvation Army Headquarters, and so I applied.

My friend happened to pop in before I left and, because I was dressed in a suit she said, "Wow, you look smart!"

I told her about the interview. She's very intuitive and said, "Yes, this is your job."

"I know," I replied because I could feel it too, "but it makes no sense. It's what I did when I was sixteen." It felt so similar to when I'd left school and had gone to work in a bank.

I went for the interview, which went well and they said they'd let me know that afternoon. On arriving home I received an e-mail from another friend entitled 'This is what you're looking for.' It was a local coach that I knew, who was looking for someone to organise and manage her business twenty hours a week. Exactly what I had thought and had been saying I wanted. Yet my whole body and intuition was guiding me towards the Salvation Army. I rang my intuitive friend and said, "Hey, I'm just ringing for an ego check," and proceeded to tell her about the new opportunity. "That's your ego," she said, and I knew she was right. As soon as I hung up the phone it immediately rang again. It was the HR lady from the Salvation Army calling to say they'd like to offer me the job. I said yes.

It still made no logical sense to me and I felt like I had made no progress at all in my years since leaving school. My role was to input all the financial data for all the areas' different Salvation Army churches. That first afternoon I nearly burst out laughing; as I picked up the information for one of the churches in my home town of Bristol I noticed that the lady in charge was my first ever boss when I worked in the bank at sixteen. 'Now you're really having a laugh.' I chuckled inwardly to the wisdom.

I thoroughly enjoyed working at the Salvation Army Headquarters. Not for the work, I felt accomplished with it after the first week, but the people were amazing. It felt like being in a wonderful womb of Love, a place to replenish and grow strong again. I loved chatting about my experiences and hearing their take on it. Gradually, I began to see that some of them knew of the Love of God, rather than simply the wrath of God, which had been my block to God and organised religion. I attended some of their church meetings and also began studying the Bible. Some of it made sense to me but some of it didn't. Some of it I felt had been misinterpreted and misunderstood – translated through the limited awareness of humans rather than the cosmic loving presence. Yet it got me using the word 'God' which before was something I had a strong aversion to. I had never believed in a vengeful, punishing God, a God of judgement and retribution, a world of sinners; it just simply felt wrong.

I had previously referred to the Loving Presence as The Universe or Source. I don't think the name really matters. The important thing is what we mean by it. I also think it's not something you can understand with your intellect. Instead it is something that you know through direct experience. When I use the word God I am referring to that Unconditional Love that is the power source for the creation of all things.

I enjoyed my exploration of God at the Salvation Army, but Christianity and the Bible was just not quite 'it' for me. As much as I wholeheartedly agree with many of the basic premises of Christianity and now know many gorgeous Christians, I guess what it did was melt down some more of my old judgements and ideas.

About a month into working at the Salvation Army I received an e-mail from the University asking if I was going to return to my degree. I was surprised because I thought I had left it too long. I immediately contacted them to find out whether I could return. I was informed that the decision was down to the Dean of the Psychology Department and that I needed to write and explain my circumstances to request a return. I did this and was delighted to be accepted back onto the programme to finish my final year. I would re-start in October.

April 2012

It's like waking up from a dream. It happens in a flash and is accompanied with this thought/realisation of, 'Shit, I fell asleep again and I didn't even notice,' and an overwhelming sense of peace takes centre stage. It's a bit like being in two places at once. I am still fully aware of the vacuum cleaner in my hand as it sucks at the landing carpet; only suddenly it seems so much more fun! And I am simultaneously aware of my awareness being in a resting place beyond just this physical reality. The colours of the world are brighter and I feel totally alive, vibrant and exuberant! I get a sense that this expanded awareness has a birds-eye view of my life and if I can surrender it will guide me every step of the way. Whereas, if I want to direct my life I am doing it from ground level and cannot ever possibly see everything that makes up the whole scenario of any given event or experience. Words sadly fail to capture the essence of this divine experience, but it is like a remembrance that the world is far more than I had previously thought. It is a divine dancing elegance; a living, breathing, pulsating oneness. I float in a sea of bliss. An enormous smile lights my face, a grin that just won't subside. It's a bit like the feeling of being 'in love,' only heightened and more divine. Everything is alive; everything is being breathed, pulsed and brought to life by the one beating heart.

My immediate thought is that I want to hold this forever and I don't want to return to the slumber. I watch this thought invade the blissful space and surrender to it totally; what will be, will be. I have woken before only to fall back to sleep. A background thought of being isolated, being alone and needing to connect with someone attempts to penetrate the peace. I think of Ro and there is a sense of urgency that I need him in some way. I have had this decoy many times before and I say a prayer to God, reaffirming my wish to absolutely surrender my separate self.

Melting further into the experience, gratitude and peace fall in me like gentle snowflakes. I focus on the breath and the growing sense of expansion and bliss.

This state exists for about an hour before it is time to collect Martha from school. I feel fragile in this state, vulnerable and wide open somehow. As I'm driving I pass some parked cars on my left and the person coming towards me swerves slightly into my path. Perhaps they were thinking that I should have waited for them rather than carried on. It makes me jump and it triggers fear. My body tenses and my thoughts become fearful. This world is a horrible place full of angry people. Fear churns in my solar plexus. The barrage of negativity continues... 'I am alone. No one loves me, no one understands and so it is better to remain where I was with how life is.' For a brief moment fear is on the verge of victory when I suddenly remember to watch. I take a breath. I embrace the churning in my solar plexus. 'It is just fear,' I remind myself. 'It's the opposite.' I say another prayer, yet again reaffirming my choice to completely surrender my separate self. Out loud I say, "I choose God, I choose Oneness, I choose Love."

The desperate sense that I need someone continues to nag away. I do not want to go here, to this new place. I do not want to be on my own. Suddenly the thought occurs that this is just another little ruse from the tireless clutches of my separate self. I allow this thought to permeate and, again, just observe. Maybe Ro is simply a distraction in the arsenal of separation. I watch the mistrust begin to bubble, the rising paranoia. This time around, far from being in 'ITS' clutches, it is simply observed and very quickly lays down its snapping head. I remind myself that I am not doing any of this 'waking up;' God has it handled and all I need to do is remember that I am not alone. I have never been alone and I *could* never be alone.

The place that I have been slumbering in is the place of fear. All the fearful thoughts are merely attempts for me to remain in this all-too-familiar state. I do not know what is beyond my old awareness; I have merely savoured magical moments before fear clutched me back. This time I make a vow to go forwards and I make a vow to carry on. But, how? Surely I need someone to help me? I need Ro. I need him to reveal himself. This sense of urgency and frustration stays with me for a while. I simply let it be. Watching it, allowing it. Suddenly, BAM! Laughter, release, insight. All I need is God and God quite brilliantly will create anything else that I need. I do not know what is best for me right now but I trust that God does. Again, I pray. I let go of Ro. He will play the perfect role and *I* will play the perfect role. All 'I' am required to do is to keep surrendering to God. Keep trusting God. It is not God who left me; it is me who left God.

Awakening seems like a dalliance as I tiptoe towards its embrace, then immediately turn on my heel and run away. Yet each time the experience of expansion arises, my trust in it expands and the boundaries of reality shift. The idea of making it permanent or attempting to hold it has subsided and has been replaced by a sense of 'what will be, will be.' I love it when the wisdom is with me and enjoy every moment, but when it fades I no longer strive for it to return, for I have noticed that the more I relax and just allow things to be as they are, the quicker it seems to reappear.

The remainder of the year continued fairly peacefully. I continued to enjoy working for the Salvation Army. Katy, Amy and Martha were all well and in October I began studying for my final degree year. It was a delight to be back at University and I loved being back in the learning environment.

In November, A Course in Miracles (ACIM) appeared in my life, wrapped up in a man that I fancied. I had known about ACIM for many years but had huge resistance to it because I knew it was based on forgiveness. The idea of one human being forgiving another made me feel uncomfortable. I saw it as somehow condescending and almost arrogant in some way. Anyway, call me shallow but because I fancied this guy and he was totally into it I thought I'd take a look. As I started to read and study it I found myself being filled with joy. It made the most sense out of anything else that I had come across. It fitted with the experiences of expansion that I had been having. It fitted with the way when I connected with 'the wisdom,' I would see things differently with Love and kindness. It spoke of the root cause of suffering being our separation from God and that, because of this separation that we had chosen, we felt tremendous unconscious guilt. It spoke of all the crazy ways that the 'separate mind' (Ego) functions in order to maintain the separation and therefore the suffering. It made more sense than anything else I had ever read before.

In the introduction it says: *'The Course does not aim at teaching the meaning of Love, for that is beyond what can be taught. It does aim, however, at removing the blocks to the awareness of love's presence, which is your natural inheritance.'*

I came to love the prayers, giving thanks to God, to Jesus. Initially I resisted these as my invisible barriers to organised religion were built on some pretty solid foundations. Although softened by my time at the Salvation Army, they still existed. However, one day I decided I had nothing to lose. I had read a sentence in ACIM that struck me extremely deeply.

It said: '*...realise that you must already have decided not to be wholly joyous if that is how you feel.*' (5: VII: 6).

Basically, it means if you don't feel good then you are choosing that. Really? It certainly doesn't seem like that on the surface. There are always plenty of reasons and justifications from the outside world as to why I feel how I feel.

This sentence stayed with me all day and I began to wonder if, in my resistance to not doing the practices/prayers, I was somehow reinforcing the blocks to the awareness of Love's presence. Therefore I would be unwittingly keeping Love away from myself. In that moment, however, I decided I had nothing to lose and would give it a go.

I decided to do a Google search for images of Jesus and use it as a focal point for my thoughts. I found one I really liked. It was Jesus sitting on a rock and meditating; very tranquil and peaceful. It made me smile and feel happy. Perhaps it looks nothing like Jesus, the truth is it doesn't matter. What is important is that I had discovered I had some decision over the focus of my mind and the pictures proved to be a powerful tool for me. Whenever I found myself feeling flat or negative I would take a look at what I was thinking. Unsurprisingly it was usually negative. I found that if I tried to think positive thoughts instead, that was quite hard, but if I focused on my image of Jesus and filled my thoughts with that, in no time at all I would be feeling fantastic, filled with Love. I found that my mind would become completely peaceful.

I combined the focus of my thoughts on Jesus with these three statements:

'Please fill my mind with your mind.
Please flood me with your Love.
Please help me see with your eyes.'

I cannot begin to tell you how many times this has brought me to absolute peace, insight and understanding in the face of suffering or challenge. I use this all the time and it really does create miracles in the mind. Suffering arises when we argue with how life is, thinking that it should be other than it is, whereas instant peace arises when you accept what is. The 'is-ness' of life is where your peace is, so just give up the fight.

It is very difficult to accept 'what is' when we are approaching the world with our limited human perspective; however, when you invite expansion into your mind you begin to see the world very differently. There is a wonderful forgiveness exercise where you imagine Jesus and see in your mind's eye the light. You then imagine in your mind's eye any person or situation that is currently challenging you or feels unresolved from the past, and then wrap them/it in the light.

What I learned was that resentment, bitterness, blame and any of the other negative emotions that we hold about past experiences only serve to keep us stuck. They exist as the elements of separation. We try to make sense of them through the stories that we tell about the world. They seem very real to us and we are often hugely attached to them as 'facts,' but they are not facts, they are fiction. If you truly and earnestly desire total freedom and peace then you have no choice but to decide to shift your attention and focus. You will not ever find real peace while you search with your intellect. You will only ever find real peace when you gift yourself a different point of view.

These days I think there is still so much that I do not understand about life. So much is beyond my comprehension and understanding that all I'm really interested in is... does it work? And you can't know that unless you practically have a go for yourself.

When I was at the Salvation Army one of the awesome officers had told me a story about a lady called Corrie Ten Boom. She was Jewish and had been a prisoner of war as a girl. She had somehow managed to smuggle a Bible in with her and had read it continuously the whole time that she was a prisoner. She had found an incredible faith and was so filled with forgiveness that when she got released she went round speaking about forgiveness. At one speaking event a man came up to her afterwards and said that he couldn't believe that he was forgiven for what he had done. As he put his hand out to shake hers she realised that he was one of the initial guards she had first seen when she was taken into the prisoner of war camp and stripped naked. Her hand was stuck by her side and wouldn't move. Rather than blaming the man, she immediately asked Jesus to forgive her for her inability to forgive and to help her forgive. She said that all of a sudden she was completely flooded with love and her hand came up from her side and shook the man's hand.

What I was beginning to understand and experience was that, what was needed for us as humans to solve the challenges in this world, was nothing outside of us but instead *in*side of us. This is because the problems we perceive are caused by the mind, our thoughts and beliefs. When we seek to make changes in the outside world, it is futile. It's a bit like yelling at the TV and expecting something to change. The difficulty being that we cannot make changes to the intellect with the intellect, or as Einstein said, 'You can't solve problems with the same level of thinking that created them.' Makes sense, doesn't it? Therefore we need a new way. Your job or role is to make the decision for Love. Your mind being returned to Love is done for you. You just have to be willing to allow it to happen.

Yet, what I could see in myself was a huge resistance to Love. I would glimpse it, revel in its beauty but then somehow unconsciously run away again. I gave up trying to understand why and instead started applying the forgiveness practices from ACIM. The forgiveness exercise is powerful and it's also great to extend it to you, because our self-punishment poses a huge challenge. It's so bizarre isn't it, that we keep Love from ourselves? The course describes this as simply the functioning of the separate mind, which is insane.

It's very difficult to escape this insanity, especially when we feel hurt and wounded by someone else's behaviour. What I began to witness time and again was that it worked. If I couldn't forgive I didn't give myself a hard time, but instead just acknowledged that I was still angry or hurt and that I was not ready to let it go just yet. Just knowing that it was the ONLY way and not only in my best interests, but everyone's best interests. Therefore, I would simply ask for help and keep repeating the exercise.

Perhaps you may be struggling with the idea of Jesus and God, like I used to. That's okay. If it's a step too far right now then substitute whatever works for you. For example, you could think of Source and a golden ball of light.

There is more than one way. I share this way because it is the most powerful I have found so far, to both maintain and return to that state of expanded awareness, peace and Unconditional Love.

March 2013

Love is beyond form

I've just had a shower and am drying my hair when the Oneness alights once more. As it begins to take me I put up a fight. The thought arises... 'This is a strange and unknown place that I am being taken to.' For a moment I begin to believe it but then another thought arises of, 'This hidden place is what I truly am and so therefore I must know it better than I know this world of separation.' Good point, I think. A sense inside me tells me this is true. The expansion begins again, like a deepening breath that knows no fill.

Ro is my next thought and questions cram my mind. Why won't he speak to me? Why can't we be friends? Will he ever come back to me? As despair creeps to the edges of my joy I decide to mentally take a step back and, instead of getting swept up in these thoughts, I just let them be with a thought of, 'Oh, there's that old pattern of distraction.' "Good one," I say out loud while chuckling at the severely compelling nature of my thoughts of Ro. They grab me every time, like an involuntary moth towards a bright light. As I'm watching I ponder the validity of a special someone and the needs of form; the need to be with, the need to possess. It dawns on me that Love is formless and that the Love I feel for Ro is wonderful. I question the validity of thought and ponder if it is perhaps simply an idea of separation, one that creates fear. I know the joy of Being and how blissfully happy I can feel and it becomes wholly obvious that it is not dependent on the outside world. I think it is something that arises from within, although that's not wholly accurate. There is no within as there is no without. I watch the switch of language that happens in this state, for it is no longer accurate to refer to 'me' or 'I' for I do not exist in isolation. I becomes we, for we are one. We are connected – we make up the whole.

This is not to say that we cannot and should not have intimate and exclusive relationships. Relationships are the most joyous thing in this world and offer us the opportunity to learn to love without conditions, preconceptions or agendas. When we Love in this way it is beautiful and all are free. However, I think we need to get really honest with ourselves as to whether the relationships we are in are based on Love or Fear; the distinction can be incredibly subtle.

April 2013

Things haven't worked out with my ACIM chap. I had felt really ready to commit to another person rather than secretly waiting for Ro to return. A little tip when someone tells you they are not ready for a relationship – gracefully back off and leave them to it. Oh, the gifts of hindsight. This chap did tell me he wasn't ready for a relationship but I pursued it anyway. I guess I should feel privileged that he even entertained the idea, but unfortunately it meant a few rocky months of him being unsure whether he wanted to be with me or not. He would come towards me only to withdraw and it inevitably left me feeling a bit confused. The third time he withdrew I decided to let him go. It seemed odd to me that I was choosing someone who did not know whether they wanted to be with me or not. It was suddenly obvious that I was still perhaps on some level not ready or wanting a relationship just yet. It was a very mature ending and I felt no bitterness towards him. I did feel a little sad though and some niggling little gremlins started to whisper about how I was not wanted.

When I went to bed that night I asked to be shown what it was about. I said, "I'm so tired of this, bored of this game. Show me what it's really about." In the morning as I stepped into the shower I had the sudden realisation that I was scared to be alone. Simultaneously I experienced the revelation that I can never be alone. Love flooded through my system and spontaneous joy arose. I knew instantly that the love I had spent my life searching for outside of myself existed perfectly within me. The feeling was amazing, exactly like being in love except there was no significant other to falsely attribute the credit to. The futile and exasperating search was over.

I had spent my whole life looking for that special someone to complete me. Yet I could see so clearly that this desire was born of need and not Love. That I was looking for someone to fill the void inside myself but the only thing that can do that is God. Then we Love, truly Love. Then we Love unconditionally, without the need to possess or control another. From this state we can share amazing relationships filled with Love because the supply of this Love is the never-ending supply of Unconditional Love from

God/The Universe/Source, call it what you will. Resting in that Unconditional Love we fall in Love with life itself. We welcome every single part of ourselves without judgement or criticism so that we are truly free. It is then that we can Be Love, which allows us to Love and be Loved. It is then that we find the beloved.

August 2013

Today I woke up and the whole world dissolved. I experienced my being as mind and not body. I was listening to the beginning of A Course in Miracles on audio whilst cleaning. I heard and realised so many things that I had not heard before, even though I have listened to the recording on several occasions. I was first reminded of the line, 'Heaven is a state of mind with no need.' When I experience myself as mind rather than a body then naturally of course, there is no need. How can there be? We are ethereal and perfect with no need for food, shelter or clothing. No need for Love because that is what I am. In this awareness, all needs are immediately met. There is a line which I adore and it says, 'Infinite patience produces immediate effects.'

This earthly life is a belief in a bunch of lies, a bunch of untruths about who and what we are. They run so deep. I also understand why waking up is a journey. The fear created by the shock of it would otherwise be completely detrimental. It is necessary to gradually awaken, little by little; the baby steps in the changes of the mind. It is a bit like learning a new language or a new skill. It builds as we practice until gradually it becomes fluent.

How do we come to this experience? For that is the only real way out. You cannot intellectually know it; you cannot understand the world by breaking it down into separate little parts. Knowing arises from realisation and is probably better described as a remembering. It is something in the distance that you can see clearly but not quite make out. Life itself is too vast to fathom and so, give yourself a break and let that intellectual need go. Allow the desire to understand the complexity to dissolve completely; this is where you somehow remember.

I am unsure whether there is anything I can do to create this state. It seems to arise in its own good time. I do know that the more I pursue it the more it eludes me. When I am desperate for peace, all that seems to happen is that more unrest is created. However, when I give up and don't care if I feel unrest for ages, miraculously, peace appears. (Oh, the gift of simply allowing whatever is arising). I do believe that it is what I am. What you are. What we are.

Sadly, we often do not receive the unconditional Love and affection we need as children to become whole, complete adults. Lack of Love causes deep unconscious pain, which is overwhelming to a young child and therefore, it unfortunately gets hidden by various protective strategies. A quiet desperate search begins and a vicious circle of pain is created. This is because Love is so longingly needed and yet it is coupled with a deep-seated mistrust; so even though others will show up to Love us, unconsciously we push that love away or sabotage it.

It doesn't matter what hand your childhood dealt you. It's never too late to become part of a loving family. Love is everywhere and available from many people. It doesn't just have to be your immediate blood family or intimate partner. We can find family anywhere, at any point and time when we fully allow ourselves to receive the gift of Love.

As the veil of separation dissolves, my family grows every day. My family is ever expanding because the truth is we are One family. We are the family of humanity and, a bit like bees; life is sweeter when we work as a team.

If I look back on my life with the old ideas of what I used to think was the point of life, it looks like a train wreck! However, when I view it from under the lens of Learning to Love I see the most beautiful journey unravelling. I have been learning what Love really is and learning to Love fearlessly, unconditionally and wholeheartedly. It is true that we cannot fully love another until we love ourselves. It starts with us, with you and me, and together through self-love and appreciation WE *WILL* CHANGE THE WORLD by changing ourselves! What may be more accurate is to say that the world will change because we *are* changed.

In the past I have quite literally tied myself in knots of insanity by attempting to make sense of the many experiences I have had that go beyond what I would have called normality. The thing is, both worlds seem equally real to me right now; I am as much in one as I am in the other. Sometimes I forget my connection and get caught up in the doing of life before I remember to stop and smell the roses. Then to breathe properly, take some time out, go for a walk, commune with nature, have a laugh, dance or just wiggle about a bit... any of these help. Then I re-experience that peace is found beyond my chattering monkey mind. Peace, joy and inspiration are all found in the moment.

It's quite simple really and yet the hardest thing ever. You see, we are evolving. We are changing as a species. The dynamic change is indeed happening. I could never quite make sense of it all and I ran through so many emotions I really didn't know what to do.

You see, for me, once I experienced that there was indeed more to life than simply one lifetime, than simply survival of the fittest, than simply reproducing, life began to make less and less sense. Another metaphorical map of the world suddenly discovered to be wrong. I tore it up but was left in limbo. The intellect doesn't like limbo; it only likes an organised and planned strategy. The intellect doesn't like to wander aimlessly and bumble along through life, moment to moment. Its strengths are organisation – it's linear in fashion and very set in its ways! So, can we change? The answer to this is again, actually very simple... the answer is that we have no choice and no say in the matter. Yes, we *can* and *will* change. What do we do about it? How do we make this natural transition as easy as possible on ourselves? Another simple, yet often most challenging answer – learn to go with the flow. Just what do we mean by 'go with the flow?' We as humans have a tendency to think of surrender as a weakness. I guess we link it back to images of war which, let's face it, we've done a lot of, and – quite frankly – it's time we stopped doing it. It's daft. Just what are we fighting over? Religion, politics, ideas? Fundamentally, we are fighting over ideas when you think about it. I'm right and you are wrong.

The reality is we ARE evolving, BUT we cannot take our selfishness and greed with us. It's impossible. If you do not grow you will suffer; not because you need to suffer but simply because you are refusing to change. You are stuck in a habit that you refuse to give up. It's like going to a foreign land where you do not speak the language and are refusing to learn it. No one else speaks your language; you can attempt to change everyone else to suit your needs, but that's going to be one serious uphill battle! The easiest and simplest approach is to immerse yourself by learning the new language. It would not take you long to learn enough to be able to get by and then it would just continue. Before long you would be more involved and then communicating with ease. So, we could approach this shift as the planet's new language.

At various times in life we are all called upon to learn a new way of being, a new way of communicating and a new way of living. At this time we are called to Love. We have no choice but to follow suit because it is the evolution of life itself. It is on its own course and far from us being the creators or dictators of life. Life is the one in charge. So make it easy on yourself; sit back, chill out and enjoy the ride. Start to allow yourself to become, once more, realigned with the natural flow and rhythm of life. Life beats its own drum... listen. You'll be glad you did.

As I type this I have a beaming smile on my face. Why? Because I have been resisting this inevitable shift and I'm just coming to realise in the last few weeks that it is happening by itself. You see, I thought there was something I should do, something we should all do to save the planet, but all we have to do is listen. How glorious is that? Listen and then follow the flow that starts to pour forth through you. This is your zone of genius, as Gay Hendricks calls it, 'your innate creativity expressing itself.' Beautiful. Everything that needs to happen for harmony to be restored *will* happen with ease when we allow the divine inspiration to guide us. All is perfect in God's plan.

There's a song called *Breaking Up is Hard to Do.* Well, I reckon 'Waking up is hard to do.' It's the biggest war of them all and has been going on forever. Thank God... it's time for it to end.

Chapter 13
Out of the Shadows

December 2013

As the end of the year approached I knew it was time to make a decision about what to do regarding employment. I'd now completed my degree and had contemplated going further with that, either doing a PhD or training in a psychological wellness role. Either didn't appeal to me though because I felt that I didn't want to break the world down into smaller parts in an attempt to understand it. It seemed to me that what I was looking for was actually being offered to me through ACIM and that was about expansion into Oneness, not contraction into further separation.

I didn't really want to return to the confines of a full-time employed role either but I knew that I wanted to find a way to share what I had learned. I just wasn't sure of the direction to take. I said out loud to God, "I'll do whatever you want me to do for the next twelve months," and did my best to let go and trust.

I joined a women's community which encouraged me to get back out there in the world with what I had learned and what I felt inspired to share. This was to help people find lasting peace and joy by entering the flow of life and welcoming the Loving Presence/God into their minds and hearts. Fundamentally, this is about a shift in consciousness from fear to love. I know that I am being guided to share this and that there is a loving presence/awareness working through me to do this. The thing is, I keep repeatedly getting in the way, although I perpetually do my best to surrender. I've been working on surrender since 2010 (funny how those two words don't really go together, isn't it?) Perhaps I could say I've been playing with the idea of surrender. I've discovered I'm a 'work in progress,' and I learn all the time.

I re-published my book *Process and Prosper* and launched an on-line Spiritual Development Community called Triple A. It stands for Awake, Alive, and Aware. I also began working with people to help them master The 7 Step Process contained in the book. This work makes me so happy. It fills me with absolute joy and I find the sense of connection wonderful. It's my favourite place/space to be, to watch people come to life before my very eyes by establishing their own connection with the Loving Presence/God, it is truly a blessing. To have people share with me that they are also experiencing peace and Love is so amazing.

When I think too much I lose it. When I get too future-focused I lose it. Not that it can ever really be lost because it is there all the time. It's perhaps more accurate that some sort of veil or mist blocks my view. There is nothing wrong with goals or plans but Life/God seems to have a better idea than I do as to what will make me at my most happiest. I easily forget this and take hold of the reins again and start to steer.

Life was good. I was happy. But one thing was still missing.

I would love to find a wonderful man to share with, care with, explore with, play with, grow with, love with and do great stuff with.

September 2014

I thought it was a bit of a joke, this day course called The Catch© with Sheila Beck-Reynolds. My lovely friend Jo had invited me to come with her and it was on my birthday. The girls were all away so I thought, 'Why not? It'll be a giggle.' It's always fun to spend time with Jo anyway.

The Catch© was a system created by Sheila to help you find your perfect partner in six weeks or less. I have to confess I was quite sceptical as I went along. It was an utterly brilliant day nevertheless and I really enjoyed all that she shared from her own journey in finding her partner. I particularly liked that she said that it all starts with 'you' being in a good place and loving yourself. She recommended books and exercises to help you find yourself. We went through a variety of exercises and one I really enjoyed was a meditation.

During the meditation I realised that I was still holding on to Ro and still waiting for him to come back. I'd tried all manner of things to 'let go' – cutting cords, asking, trying, and praying – the list goes on. There was such a deep bond between us; I guess it was hardly surprising that part of me was still refusing to accept it was over. Not only a very deep, shared love and the bond of a child, but also the event of the near death experience. It was his hand that stopped me from dying. More than all of that though was the fact that it was him I came back to be with. He was the reason I chose not to go, and yet, here we were apart. It made no sense.

However, during the meditation I made the decision to let him go. I just wanted him to be happy and I totally accepted that that might not be with me. I thought that, maybe with someone else he would be happier and that was okay. I could also see that all the time I was holding on to the idea of his return I was energetically blocking anyone else from coming to me. So, I decided to let go. All of a sudden in my mind's eye I saw this infinite glorious lake. I was standing on the shore and Ro was in a golden boat. He was standing up in the middle of the boat and it was floating away from me and into the distance. We were both smiling and waving to each other. Waving goodbye. It felt good and I felt content.

I left the course having enjoyed a brilliant day. The next day I wrote a letter about the qualities in my perfect partner/soul mate. I decided I had nothing to lose and it was worth a go. I spent an evening writing my letter, considering all aspects of life and relationships. I wrote it out by hand, dated it and then put it away. I thought I was relaxed about it, but at the end of the six weeks when 'he' hadn't materialised, I realised I had been waiting and on the lookout. Because the six weeks was up I let go. This felt good. I started to wonder if I would ever be in a committed intimate relationship again. Maybe that, in this lifetime I had had my share of being a couple and maybe there was a different plan for me. I didn't want to settle, I wanted to be connected on all levels, physical, mental, spiritual and emotional. If it wasn't the whole deal I would rather be on my own. I also knew that I loved the feeling of being in flow and sharing about God, about the Loving Presence that is there for us. Sharing about Jesus and the powerful impact that had on returning my mind to peace and returning me to joy when I felt out of sorts. I was also aware of my reservations about sharing this, not being religious, yet it really felt like my mission. So maybe this was my life path.

Wouldn't it be amazing if we could have Faith that was not tied to any particular religion or doctrine? If Faith was more than a belief or idea, for instance. If it was instead the very real experience of God/The Creator/Universe/Love (whatever other names you choose to give it). Perhaps some sort of free-flowing celebration of life and unity.

19th February 2015

I chose to let go of the search for love. Instead I chose to trust that 'all is well' and 'all is perfect just as it is.' If I was meant to be with someone I would; I'm not, therefore that's how it is right now. It's so hard to let go of the longing for union. I think it's one that runs deep within us.

I found my peace by acknowledging that I wanted it but by being prepared to trust life. I find that there is always immediate peace when I stop arguing with what is in any given moment, when I accept it just as it is.

I believe that Love is the answer, but opening the mind to allow Love is the greatest challenge we face.

20th February 2015

Today in our 'All of You' group we held a wonderful ceremony to honour the feminine, to honour woman and women.

It struck me at one point that it was useless to wait for anyone else to do it, rather *I* had to do it. I had to honour the feminine in me. Then I could honour the feminine in the world.

I wasn't raised with the feminine being honoured. I was raised to believe that the feminine was weak and pathetic. Something to be despised not cherished. When I was young I remember my father saying in a derogatory way, "A woman's power is between her legs." What I got from him was that women had some sort of power over men and were sirens, luring men into their trap. I remember seeing the Disney cartoon of The Hunchback of Notre Dame with my daughters; the interaction between the characters Frollo and Esméralda made me think of my dad and his view of women. Frollo is celibate (my dad obviously wasn't) and Esméralda raises passion and lust in him, which he projects out onto her and considers her a temptation sent by the devil. Yet the lust is his.

This represented many years of abuse, mistreatment and disrespect for women. Yet today I could see that the healing will not arrive whilst we fight the outside and expect it to change. The healing will come when we look deep inside and see that we women carry the same stories and ideas. We need to change our minds about the feminine, to focus on cherishing and adoring it. For when I love and adore myself, then I allow another to love and adore me.

21st February 2015

Romance arrived, how funny! I tell you, this 'letting go' thing is powerful. The difficult bit being it's so easy to convince yourself you have let go when you actually haven't. I also think we're so conditioned to hold on that it's like trying to learn a new habit. I forget that it's the only practice to do. My mind doesn't seem to like the simplicity of it and instead repeatedly attempts to convince me that I need to *do* something.

This evening I was chilling out on the sofa watching a movie, feeling utterly peaceful and content, when my phoned beeped with a Facebook message. It was my friend David from the US. I'd known David for about six months and we'd had several lengthy conversations on Skype over that period. We were always chatting about spirituality and how it appeared in our lives, sharing our journeys so far. The chats were always easy and fun. We laughed a lot and he shared many beautiful stories about his experiences which I loved hearing. I had a strong sense of connection with him that felt very lovely.

This message though, was different from the usual, 'Hey, how are you today?'

The message instead said, 'I hope you don't mind me asking you this, but I can't believe you're single. Are you open to a relationship?'

I replied that I was but that the right person hadn't showed up yet. He went on to ask me what I was looking for. I spoke from my heart and shared what I was looking for. He said he was looking for the same.

We then continued to have a wonderful conversation, which ended up with him saying, 'You're welcome here any time.'

'Thank you,' I replied. 'It's a bit tricky with the girls though. You're always welcome to visit here.'

'Great,' he typed. 'When?'

Blimey! I got my diary and checked to see when I could create some free time. 'How about 21st March?' I suggested.

'Brilliant,' he replied. 'I'll check here and let you know – then I'll book a flight. I'm so excited to meet you in person.'

'Me too,' I replied, with a beaming smile on my face.

The next day David messaged me to say he could arrive on Monday 24th March. We agreed for how long he would stay and he said he'd book his flight. I was really excited and looking forward to meeting him. We both agreed to put no pressure on it. Even though we both felt very drawn to each other, it's a whole different thing in the flesh, isn't it? Physical chemistry seems to have a mind/life of its own, you can't manufacture it… it's just there or not. My thinking was that we got on really well with lots in common, and so would have a fabulous time even if the romance didn't quite pan out.

That night he messaged me to confirm he had booked his flight and then said, 'I'm quite the romantic. I once fell for a girl in North America. I flew up to see her and when I arrived she'd got back with her ex-boyfriend. So if anything like that happens just let me know and save me the flight.'

I chuckled at this, having been single for such a long time I felt sure nothing like this would happen.

We continued to speak every single day. It was lovely to feel really close to him and I grew more excited about his visit. We were busy planning what we would do and the places I would take him to. He adored nature and there are so many beautiful places to go where I live, it was hard to narrow it down. The girls agreed it was exciting too which was great, and our house was looking forward to our American visitor.

Chapter 14
Home at Last

20th March 2015

David is due to arrive on Monday. I'm still so excited and can't wait to see him. We've grown quite close over the last four weeks and have shared deeply a lot of our thoughts. It seems like all the talking is done now, as for the last week we have run out of things to say. We just want to spend some quality time with each other now. This week seems to have gone by quite slowly. A bit like waiting for Christmas when you're young.

This evening I received a text from Ro.

'Got some news that will change Martha's visits,' it said.

I really thought he was happy and, being in such a joyous state myself, texted back,

'Marriage? Baby?'

'No. The opposite,' was the reply.

Oh! He asked if we were around in the morning and said he would like to come and see us. He said he'd come and take us out for breakfast.

I decided not to let my mind run away with itself and instead wait and see what he wanted to say. Let's face it – last time he was heading off with someone else, so perhaps the same thing was happening again. Maybe I was nothing to do with it.

21st March 2015

Well! That's thrown a spanner in the works.

Ro arrived to take Martha and I out as he promised. He came in for a cup of tea first. He told me that he had split up with his girlfriend, and then he spent some time chatting to Martha by himself to tell her. She wasn't too bothered or upset, so that was good.

As we headed into town for breakfast, Martha in the back and myself in the front passenger seat, he glanced over at me and said,

"Still got that same chemistry between us!" in a really flirty, playful way.

I could also feel the chemistry because, to be honest, it was hard not to. I looked over at him and raised my eyebrows saying,

"Easy, tiger. Your timing sucks!"

Breakfast was fun. I always adored being around him. There is something contagious in his energy; something that made me feel very alive. I still adored him, but I knew that anyway, and it didn't necessarily mean anything.

After the meal we headed back to mine because Martha had arranged to meet up with her friend. This left Ro and I some time to talk. He told me that he wanted to see if there was still anything between us because he had been feeling discontented. When he reflected on what he wanted, it always came back to me.

I informed Ro about David's imminent arrival and he said that he did not come to get in the way of anything I was doing, and that it was fine for me to carry on with David if that's what I wanted. He said he didn't know for sure what he wanted but did feel drawn to explore whether there was still anything between us.

We talked throughout the morning, and at one point he went to give me a kiss. It was funny because my whole body reacted before my mind had engaged and I held him at arm's length.

"You can't do that," I informed him.

"Why not?" he asked.

"Because I'm not ready for that," I admitted. My head was unclear and I didn't want to compromise myself in any way. The last thing I wanted to do was create any sense of guilt that would cloud my judgement.

"Sorry," he said.

Thankfully, I had already arranged to see Jo that afternoon, which was perfect. I try my best not to do drama these days but sometimes I just need an, 'Oh my god, this has happened' moment. Jo was brilliant and said *so* wisely, "Why don't you just tell David exactly what has happened?" Her suggestion was so blindingly obvious and absolutely perfect. I couldn't believe what David had said about that other lady in North America. Blimey!

David knew all about Ro because I had shared my story with him. Before we were being romantic, he had been fascinated by my near death experience, so knew of my love for Ro.

I messaged him explaining that Ro had turned up wanting to see if there was anything between us. I said that I was confused right now and so couldn't make him any promises. I finished with, 'I don't know how that makes you feel about coming over here.'

I really wasn't sure whether I wanted him to come or not. I thought I would ask how he felt about it.

Jo also said something else, which really resonated with me. She said, "That which is for you, won't go by you."

I loved this. It made me feel like I could breathe, like there was no rush to make a decision. No sense of should. There was just the opportunity to explore possibilities.

Ro had invited me to the cinema before he left at lunchtime. Amy and Martha were out with friends so I agreed. I texted Martha to say I was going to the cinema with Ro and would see her when I got home. It was funny to be 'out on a (sort of) date' with him. To be honest, I wasn't sure if we were out on a date or not. David was on my mind and I hoped he was okay. I hadn't heard anything from him at all, but I knew he was with his son and so wouldn't check his messages until he was back home.

The cinema was fun and Amy and Martha were both there when we arrived back. They were in Amy's room lying on the bed watching a film together. I went up to make sure they were alright. They were brilliant.

"Are you okay, Mum?" Amy asked. "What are you going to do? You must be really confused."

Ahhh, bless them. They are so amazing. We had a good chat about it. I asked them what they thought to which they shared that they didn't know. It was a bit weird the idea of Ro and I getting back together because we had been apart for so long. They were laughing because Martha had got home first, then when Amy arrived and asked where I was Martha had replied,

"Mum and Dad have gone to the cinema." They both said it sounded so strange – they had looked at each other and Martha said, "That sounds so weird putting Mum and Dad in the same sentence like that," before they both started laughing at the absurdity of it all.

I agreed it *was* weird and bizarre for the timing. After a while of chatting on Amy's bed I set up the spare bed for Ro in the office before departing to bed myself.

The next morning there was still no word from David. I hoped he was alright. I woke early and had a really strong urge that I wanted to lie down with Ro. Not to have sex, not to make it complicated, but just time to 'be'.

I crept downstairs and peeked in on him. He was asleep so I tiptoed back to my bed. 'Probably for the best,' I thought. I wrote in my journal and rested for a while, pondering the current situation. The urge to be with Ro was still strong and so I went downstairs again and popped my head round the door. This time he was awake, so I made us a cup of tea and sat in the chair in the office.

After a while I asked, "I'd like to lie down with you. Would that be okay?"

"That would be nice," he replied, moving over and lifting the bed covers.

In my pyjamas I climbed into the bed and we lay facing each other looking into each other's eyes. It was wonderful. No need for words, just love, just allowing. We stayed like this for quite some time and then he pulled me into his arms and smelled my hair. He held me tight and we both took a deep breath of utter contentment. It felt right in his arms.

Late morning I received a message from David. It was absolutely beautiful and confirmed to me the wonderful man that I thought he was.

It said, 'Wow. You got me with that one. Think I will stay on this side of the pond until you work things out. Good luck. Thanks for telling me. At least in this lifetime I have never known a woman to die and come back for me. I know he means this world and that one to you. I am actually more happy for you than disappointed. I hope it works out.'

What an amazing man! What a beautiful soul.

I knew that I wanted to give Ro and I the time to have a good look and see what there was between us, to see if we had a future together. David was a completely lovely man but I had spent virtually eight years longing for Ro to come back. Now that the opportunity had arisen I had to give it some space to see what was there. I knew that if I didn't I would always wonder.

I shared with Ro that David was no longer coming and that I knew I wanted to give him (Ro) and I the time and space to explore if we were what each other really wanted. He reacted with fear. I felt him contract and he said,

"Oh no, I'm going to hurt you."

I was a little surprised by this comment and felt myself withdraw slightly in self-protection, but took a deep breath and enquired,

"Would you like to clarify exactly what you mean by that?"

My senses told me that all of sudden this was real. All the time David was coming there was no pressure, but as soon as he wasn't coming that meant this was more serious.

Ro admitted he didn't know if it was right. He didn't know if it was me that he really wanted. He was worried that he would hurt me all over again by deciding that it wasn't me.

"Whoa," I said gently. "Don't run before you can walk. I know that we are simply exploring whether this is something we want to have a go at. We've got more talking to do about how it will be different and what we have learned. It's okay. Do you remember that poem I wrote called *Promise Me This*?"

"Not really," he replied honestly.

"Well, let me get it," I insisted, "Because it explains how I feel about intimate relationships and the way I am learning to be in my life."

I printed it out and read it to him:

Promise Me This

True love defies all time, all boundaries and is created to last,
So promise to never let us get trapped by the past.
Instead to see me every day with eyes anew,
This is the secret of a special few.
True love is the way to all that is dear,
Honest, caring, the pathway is clear.
Promise to listen with all of your heart,
Let's do this darling right from the start.

Promise me you'll always be open to see,
If problems arise they are in you and not in me.
That no matter what happens or what challenges we face,
You'll keep your heart open in love's true embrace.
For true love does not judge, condemn or chastise,
It doesn't demand, punish or despise.
It never says you must not do this or do that,
Or zaps your life force so that you feel flat.

Promise to share and tell me the truth,
Never to hide or be aloof.
Promise to listen and promise to say,
So that silly little problems never get in our way.
Promise to keep exploring,
So life never gets boring.
Promise to take time out just to be,
To gaze into my eyes and fully connect with me.

I do not ask you to promise to be mine forever,
On this journey of life together.
I do not ask you to ever compromise your heart,
Even if this means we must be apart.
For I will never put you in a cage,
As the story of your life unfolds on the page.
I ask this my darling for you not for me,
Because my greatest wish is that you will always be free.

Yet if we are so lucky that together we grow old,
Promise to wrap me tight in a loving hold.
Moment to moment we'll skip through this life,
Hand in hand, side by side for the joy and the strife.
For this life is amazing, filled with majesty, mystery and wonder,
When we totally let go and in true love surrender.

I love you x

I pointed out that the poem has 'I love you' on the end and chuckled. "Do you understand you are free?" I asked.

He smiled and nodded. "Thank you," he said.

The rest of the afternoon was pleasant. Ro booked a hotel near his work and left early evening to travel up there. I was pleased that he was leaving and looking forward to some time to digest what had happened. Over the next few days he sent me some nice messages. On Thursday evening I was driving up to stay overnight in Warwick for a monthly meeting the next day. I booked my hotel and then wondered if Ro was free for dinner, as I would literally be driving past his door. I messaged him and he replied saying that it would be lovely and to come and meet him in the pub near his work.

I was really nervous as I arrived. He came out to greet me as I was parking and met me with a beaming smile. After a quick drink we went to a lovely Thai restaurant. Dinner was delicious and it was wonderful to be with him. My nerves had disappeared and I was thoroughly enjoying the flirtatious vibe between us when he suddenly looked me in the eye and said,

"Don't go to your hotel. Come back with me and stay at mine."

I took a deep breath. I really wanted to but I also didn't want to. I didn't want to mess this up. I wanted to have the time to know that we were doing the right thing. The sexual chemistry between us was always strong and I didn't want this to be the guiding factor. After a while I replied, "Okay, but I'll be wearing my pyjamas."

"Okay," he smiled.

Back at the hotel we lay facing each other on the bed. So interesting, this mix of old and new. The love was palpable and his eyes divine, sparkling and intense. It felt so wonderful to be in his presence. Part of it seemed unreal, after all those years of longing, after all those dreams of being with him only to wake and feel disappointed. I almost had to pinch myself to believe that here we were in reality.

Gentle caressing led to gentle kissing. I adored being back in his arms, his exquisite touch that sent shivers down my spine and set my whole body tingling, hungry for more. Gentle kissing led to passionate kissing, periodically either one of us pulling away in an attempt not to go too far. His scent, his energy, those eyes alive with desire felt intoxicating like a drug and I felt myself succumbing. So much for wearing my pyjamas!

Ro was kissing and breathing on my neck and heavenly tickly tingles were running rampant up and down my body, heightening my pleasure and increasing my desire. I let go and allowed myself to feel every tiny bubble of erotic pleasure. He began to unbutton my blouse and kiss lower down my neck until he reached my soft breast tissue. He unbuttoned the rest of my blouse and helped my arms out before unzipping and removing my skirt. Gentle kisses and his soft breath continued to caress my chest as he unsnapped my bra and removed it too. My body was on sensitivity overdrive, it was divine. Gently he kissed his way down my body, over my tummy, over the piece of leg that is now my tummy, gently stroking and kissing my grafted skin all the way to my pubic bone before removing my underwear. Then he stopped, looked me up and down in my naked finery and said,

"My God, you ARE so beautiful!"

Before I knew it the tears pricked in my eyes and I burst into tears. He lay down beside me and wrapped me in his arms. Large, hot tears coursed down my face.

"I'm sorry," I mumbled into his chest.

"It's absolutely fine," he said.

After a while I managed to say, "I never thought you'd do that again," before a second round of large tears ran down my face.

Finally, the tears subsided and I told him about that first time I had seen my whole body in the shower in the hospital and what I had thought. He held me tight and whispered reassuringly in my ear, "I'm here now."

It felt so amazing to be with him, so right. I couldn't quite get my head round how we had lost each other before; it seemed completely absurd. I decided if it was only this moment with him then I would take it. I would enjoy it to the full and have no regrets, whatever happened next. Then we made love and curled up in each other's arms, home at last.

Epilogue

We've been back together for 18 months as I write this and we've never been happier. We moved into a beautiful new home as a family in June 2015 and got engaged in August 2016. Ro proposed on one knee at Wistman's Wood, I couldn't think of a more perfect spot. Our love continues to flourish and be appreciated. I still have to pinch myself every now and again to believe he's really here with me. I adore him as much as I always did, but the difference now is that I appreciate him and I now love myself enough to be loved, adored and cherished. I do not think that the novelty will ever wear off. I hope it doesn't and I guess I can always remind myself of the longing shared with you throughout these pages lest I ever forget.

I long for you to know that you are safe, loved and perfect just as you are. I pray that this becomes your experience of your Self.

From my heart to yours,

Go in peace, my friend.

Wendy x

I'd like to leave you with my story in poem form:

In the Face of Death

Let me start here, right at the beginning,
I'll tell you a story, a yarn I'll be spinning.
The tale of my life, the ups and the downs,
The highs and the lows, the smiles and frowns.

Not all of it's pretty, quite messy in fact,
Far from a graceful journey, more like a forest that's hacked.
I've struggled, I've fought, been angry and wanting,
Greedily feasting without care or stopping.

Wounded was I from hurts aplenty,
That left me angry, scared and feeling empty.
Going through life with a hidden desire,
To put out the blazing internal fire.

The pot of anger that simmered and grew,
The hatred, the spite that I never knew.
Existed inside and influenced my actions,
Keeping life boxed, neatly like fractions.

Separate parts kept packed away,
Silently hiding because I'd never say.
The sad thing is my spirit I crushed,
And created a life born of mistrust.

Laugh and live happy and free,
That is the way life's supposed to be.

But far from this regular fairy tale,
Sometimes life can be horribly stale.

It felt as if I was locked in a trap,
Slowly becoming a maniac.
My mind it chuntered day and night,
It built and built on all the fright.

Lonely and scared, abandoned was I,
Further confused, felt like I would die.
I put on my armour and picked up my sword,
There really seemed like no other accord.

I'll fight my way right through this life,
With my invisible sword and my invisible knife.
The sad thing is I won't even realise,
That I have donned this armour of considerable size.

Put in place to protect my heart,
Put in place right at the start.
I came here loving, soft and true,
I can here open, fresh and new.

But gradually the wounds built by the day,
Compounding, expanding and getting in the way.
It seemed the only choice was to fight,
To fight and struggle with all my might.

All donned in my armour I took up the attack,
Too scared was I to ever look back.
The trouble was the future came from the past,
Founded on my stories that I'd built to last.

Repeating the cycle went round and round,
Burying my spirit deep underground.
The power of the stories retold from the past,
Their powerful impact and holding tight fast.

It wasn't until that fateful day,
When you nearly took my life away.
As I teetered in the balance between two worlds,
Catapulted forwards a new way uncurled.

You brought me Love, you made me tingle,
Your light so bright came to intermingle.
I'd never before felt Love like this,
The only word might be bliss.

But even this is not enough,
When you try to talk of the invisible stuff.
Alive and gentle, soft and enthralling,
You wrapped me up in a Love adoring.

You melted my wounds, it felt divine,
And offered me a new lifeline.
I took that gift and back I came,
To try again without any shame.

At times it's hard not to be sucked back,
To that life lived as if a maniac.
At times I got lost, I left your warm embrace,
But you guided me back with that invisible trace.

Transmission, volition, true life sublime,
This is the life, the life that's now mine.
If I told you it was easy I'd be telling a lie.
It's been hard for me, the harder I try.

But really this is the secret, it's easy you see,
So easy to do that you won't believe me.
When I see the ease I look back and laugh,
At how hard I have made it walking this path.

For the harder I try, the harder I fall,
When I stop listening to the invisible call.
I do not know who you are,
All I know is the Love that comes from afar.

This carries me forward like wings on a bird,
Why I try and go alone is truly absurd.
I'll keep casting off my armour and laying down my sword,
So that I may live fully with your accord.

Quotation Sources

'The truth shall set you free but first it'll piss you off'
Gloria Steinem

http://time.com/36046/gloria-steinem-8-funny-quotes-80-birthday/

Prayer on page 180-181 taken from The Way of Mastery Teachings by Jeshua ben Joseph. Shanti Christo Foundation.

'The Course does not aim at teaching the meaning of Love, for that is beyond what can be taught. It does aim, however, at removing the blocks to the awareness of love's presence, which is your natural inheritance.' A Course in Miracles.

'…realise that you must already have decided not to be wholly joyous if that is how you feel.' (5: VII: 6). A Course in Miracles.

Contact Wendy

www.wendy-harrington.com

Contact Ruth

www.harringtontherapy.com

Made in the USA
Middletown, DE
08 May 2023

30256642R00151